Our battle against sin is to the death – the death not of us but of our sins – because Christ triumphed for us two thousand years ago. In his bold new book *Tap*, Yancey Arrington helps us connect with the victory of Christ right here, right now, in our lives today.

– RAY ORTLUND, JR.
Lead Pastor, Immanuel Church, Nashville,
author of *A Passion for God*

Ancient wisdom made practical. That is what Yancey Arrington has done in this book. He shows us the folly of well-meaning but ineffective sin-turning strategies. *Tap* shows us the way to really repent and prefer Christ over the sin that would seek to destroy us.

– DARRIN PATRICK
Lead Pastor, The Journey, St. Louis,
author of *Church Planter: The Man, The Message, The Mission*

With wonderful gifts of communication and great biblical insight Yancey Arrington leads us through the realities of our battle against sin and the power of gospel truth. "Belief before behavior" is not simply a slogan, it is the key to victory that Yancey uses to unlock the hope every believer needs (and has) to walk in the strength of God's grace.

– BRYAN CHAPELL
President, Covenant Seminary,
author of *Christ-Centered Worship*

Yancey Arrington extends the power of hope in the gospel to those whose fight with sin has left them tired, doubtful and defeated. With *Tap* in hand, get ready to fight well against sin instead of merely fighting hard. Get ready to believe again that Jesus made a way for you to defeat the sins that have defeated you. Get ready for a grateful love to overflow in your newly, liberated life.

– BRUCE WESLEY
Senior Pastor, Clear Creek Community Church, Houston

You won't get to the essence of your bout with sin with a more relevant and readable guide than Yancey Arrington's *Tap*. Having served alongside of Yancey in local church ministry, I can attest that this weighty, biblical wisdom is brought you by a true fighter himself.

– WILL MANCINI
Founder, Auxano
author of *Church Unique*

Many of us live in a dull stupor, forgetting that we are in a battle with sin. Yancey Arrington awakens us to the fight. Offering a biblically-guided battle plan, *Tap* trains us to trust and treasure Jesus above all else—this is the only way to victory in this ultimate fight.

– JEFF LAWRENCE
Lead Pastor, Chatham Community Church, Chapel Hill

DEFEATING THE SINS
THAT DEFEAT YOU

YANCEY ARRINGTON

CLEAR CREEK RESOURCES

Tap: Defeating The Sins That Defeat You

Copyright © 2010 by Yancey C. Arrington
Published by Clear Creek Resources

999 N. Egret Bay Blvd.
League City, Texas 77573

ISBN 978-0-9825517-9-0

Unless otherwise indicated, all Scripture quotations are taken from:

The Holy Bible: English Standard Version®, copyright © 2001 by Crossway Bibles, a division of Good News Publishers. Used by permission. All rights reserved.

All Scripture emphases have been added by the author.

Cover design: Steven Trimble

First printing, 2010.

Printed in the United States of America

DEDICATION

To my dearest wife Jennefer,
who allowed me to pursue this endeavor
through her love and support

And to my sons:
Thatcher, Haddon and Beckett,
who let Daddy leave home
every Friday during the spring
so he could write his little book

And to Clear Creek Community Church,
both home and place of grace for many years
With much patience, they have endured my teaching
yet still allow me to be one of their pastors
I can think of no better place to serve

And ultimately to the Lord Jesus Christ,
the One who has conquered for me where I have failed,
and in whose gospel I have hope, life and love
Amen.

CONTENTS

Acknowledgments   9

Introduction   13

1. Life in the Cage   17

2. Before You Enter the Cage   31

3. Holds That Don't Work   43

4. Having a Good Hold   57

5. Repenting of Repenting   69

6. Contender Repentance   81

7. Tapping Out Sin   97

Conclusion   117

Notes   121

ACKNOWLEDGMENTS

For years I had the thought I would write a book before turning thirty. Now, just shy of entering my forties, I realize that, at least for me, a book is the product of both discipline and a dream. I was not short on dreaming (I tend to dream a lot); I was lacking discipline. That was until my lovely wife Jennefer gave me a unique Christmas gift. She told me I could have every Friday to write while she would spend time with our boys. Within a few months of her gracious offer, the manuscript for *Tap* was born. Thanks Jen. I love you very much! This book would not have happened without your loving sacrifice.

I want to thank the staff of Clear Creek Community Church, especially Bruce Wesley, Mark Carden, Greg Poore and Chris Alston. They are not just fellow pastors but beloved friends and brothers. They also have been incredibly supportive of me and my writing endeavor. Serving with them has been one of the greatest gifts a pastor can be given.

Every year I spend time with some of my closest friends from college in a trip called *Fandango* (which may someday be a future book). These men are also my brothers: Jeff Lawrence, Andy Kerckhoff, Jason Ganze,

Scott James, Mitch Kramer and Craig Hasselbach. They were the first outside of my wife to read, critique and offer advice with *Tap*. I don't see that strategy changing in the future. I love you guys and am grateful God put us together years ago. *¡Viva Los Matadors!*

I would also like to thank Dr. John Hannah, Research Professor of Theological Studies and Distinguished Professor of Historical Theology at Dallas Theological Seminary. Almost immediately after I finished the basic manuscript, Dr. Hannah requested to see it. I acquiesced with much trepidation knowing him to be somewhat of an expert on John Owen. He not only graciously gave *Tap* a reading but personally recommended it to senior editors he knew at different publishing houses. I remember telling Jennefer that it didn't matter what happened to the manuscript, Dr. Hannah's kind words about it somehow made me feel like I had accomplished my mission. I still feel that way.

Deep appreciation goes to Dr. Ray Ortlund, Jr. I deeply respect Ray as a scholar, theologian and pastor, but those pale in comparison to how much I admire his personal devotion to Jesus. Ray was not only kind enough to take time out of his busy schedule to read my initial manuscript but offered wise and needed suggestions. Frankly, the better parts of chapter seven are due to Ray's wisdom, the less-than-better parts are likely due to mine.

Thanks as well to Scott Knight of Agon Ministries. One publisher tried to pair us together because of Scott's involvement with MMA. I like MMA, Scott is invested in MMA. I talk about fighters, he knows them personally. His heart to reach young men for the gospel is inspiring, and his support of my work has been a blessing. Additionally, Chuck Land has been a wonderful encouragement to me. He was one of the first friends to suggest I write this book. Thanks for the push, Chuck!

I would also like to express my deep thanks to Mandy Turner and her fantastic editing skills. Her task was very difficult: turn a speaker into a writer. Nevertheless, she volunteered immediately when I asked for manuscript editors. Almost every evening, when going over her edits, I found myself saying, "This is so much better than what I initially gave her!" The same could be said for Dawn Hastie, who graciously volunteered to proofread my work. She was even kind enough to do some editing herself. Thanks for blessing me with your time and talents. I am incredibly indebted to both these women for their gifts, intelligence and ability to go the extra mile for *Tap*.

Last but certainly not least, I am most grateful for John Owen. Had he never written *Of the Mortification of Sin in Believers* in 1656, *Tap* would not exist. I am grateful for Banner of Truth and other publishers that have sought to make this Puritan pastor's teachings available to the modern-day church. I am deeply thankful to God for Owen's ministry and insightful teaching on fighting sin so that Christ might be magnified and sin vanquished.

INTRODUCTION

I believe I can begin this book with some assumptions. I assume you love Jesus, try to honor him with your life and desire to grow spiritually. For those truths I am grateful and pray this book will aid you in your journey with Christ. But I can also make other assumptions. I assume there is likely a sin, or maybe sins, which exert such a powerful sway in your life and heart that they have relentlessly plagued you for extended seasons if not years. Unfortunately, I can sympathize with you in this. Indeed, I believe many Christians throughout the ages could commiserate with us concerning the struggle with sin. However, I think I can make one final assumption about you.

You want to defeat the sin which so easily defeats you.

If that is the case, why is it that countless numbers of Christians experience so little victory over certain sins? Surely it cannot be for lack of trying. Numbers increase every day of believers who memorize Scripture, join accountability groups and exercise other various spiritual disciplines in an attempt to escape the sins which seem to have them by the tail. Yet it seems that for many, the results are still the same, leaving them in despair and frustration. Please understand, I am not arguing that Christians should not "fight the good fight" (1 Tim. 6:12) eschewing the spiritual disciplines. We need them. They are essential in any strategy to rid our lives of sin. I am simply suggesting the reason many of us find little to no victory over sin isn't because we do not fight, but because we do not fight well.

Could that be true of you? Could it be that maybe, just maybe, the reason you do not win against sin is because you adopted the wrong strategy – where all the spiritual disciplines in the world will not help you defeat sin? Is it possible that in your battle against sin you began with an erroneous approach? Again, the question is not do you fight *hard* against sin, but do you fight *well* against sin?

This book hopefully will offer a different approach to fighting sin. It isn't a new understanding of sin-fighting; on the contrary, it has been around for some time – centuries to be exact. However, I think it will be good and wise counsel for those wanting a better strategy for defeating sin. C.S. Lewis once noted that a Christian should read at least one old book to every three new ones. He writes,

> *Every age has its own outlook. It is specially* [sic] *good at seeing certain truths and specially liable to make certain mistakes. We all, therefore, need the books that will correct the characteristic mistakes of our own period. And that means the old books.*[1]

INTRODUCTION

While there is much to celebrate about contemporary texts dealing with our fight against sin, this book will hearken back to a generation of sin-fighters gone by – a generation whose approach to fighting sin will prove a helpful and necessary corrective to many popular, but ineffective strategies today. In that sense, this is an old book.

But it is also a new book. Within these pages we will draw a parallel with a contemporary type of fighting, one done in a cage and where the conquered either taps out or gets knocked out. While the sport may be relatively new, using fighting as an illustration for instructing believers is not. The Apostle Paul frequently referred to the combat sport of his day (probably the boxing events of the Isthmian Games which were second only to the Olympics) in order to help them relate to their struggle with sin (cf., 1 Tim. 6:12, 2 Tim. 4:7, 1 Cor. 9:6). In the same spirit, this book will parallel a modern picture of fighting, not to glorify the fight, but to instruct and encourage the fighter in each of us.

Thus I commend to you, fellow sin-fighter, this *new/old* book. My prayer is that the Holy Spirit will not only reveal your possible need for a better strategy for fighting sin, but also grant you the grace to see it truly, genuinely defeated.

1
LIFE IN THE CAGE

You put the Devil on the other side, and I will come to fight.
– MMA LEGEND ROYCE GRACIE

We hope that you choke. That you choke.
– RADIOHEAD, *EXIT MUSIC (FOR A FILM)*

In an arena filled with screaming devotees, an octagon-shaped cage holds two fighters fitted with gloves about half the size of those in boxing. At the word of the referee, they begin to employ a dizzying combination of boxing skills, jujitsu, Greco-Roman wrestling, Muy Thai, and various other martial arts disciplines in order to defeat their opponent. What you are witnessing is the blossoming sport known as Mixed Martial Arts (MMA), where athletes are just as much at home fighting on the ground as they are on their feet. Watch a few matches and you'll see that, unlike boxing, MMA allows its fighters to grapple as well as punch, creating scenarios where arm bars, wrist locks and choke holds are employed to force opponents into one of four results: submission (known as a "tap out"), unconsciousness, a broken limb, or some combination of all these. This has led some critics of MMA to label it as nothing more than a "blood sport" that solely celebrates gratuitous violence. Early in the sport, it was probably a fair critique.

I watched my first MMA match in 1993, just as the sport was being introduced in America. My roommate at the time excitedly showed me a video called the Ultimate Fighting Championship (UFC) "No Rules Fighting". It would have been more accurately named "Only Two Rules Fighting" – eye gouging and biting were not legal, but everything else was fair game – groin shots, head butts, you name it.

The sport at the time was simple: two guys, no gloves, no weight classes, just *mano y mano* seeing who can survive. Ironically, the man who won the championship – a wiry 175-pound Brazilian grappler named Royce (pronounced "Hoyce") Gracie – rarely punched anyone. He regularly caused fighters twice his size to tap out in mere moments, simply by twisting them into pretzels on the mat. Overall, the matches were hardcore, to put it mildly. Blood, broken bones, and joints blown out were par for the course. I remember my roommate exclaiming, "Wow! Isn't this awesome?" I responded, "Dude, this is sick. I can't believe you watch this stuff!"

Two hours later we turned it off.

More spectacle than sport, it was deemed illegal in many states. In an effort to become more mainstream, over the last several years the UFC specifically, and MMA in general, has created stiffer rules: weight classes, illegal moves, five minute rounds, use of gloves, and so on. However, even with the implementation of all those measures, many continue to assert that the barbarism of MMA merits no cultural good.

THE RISE OF MMA

Regardless of your view, no one can deny how powerful a force MMA has become today. At the writing of this book, it is the fastest growing sport in the United States for men, particularly between the ages of 18-34 – the coveted age target for media marketing. In fact, on October 10th, 2006 more 18-34 year-old males watched UFC's Tito Ortiz vs. Ken Shamrock (1.6 million) than Major League Baseball playoff game between the Oakland A's and Detroit Tigers (1.1 million).[2]

Its increase in popularity has opened the door for MMA to enter mainstream America. It has been given a regular spot on ESPN.com, graced the cover of *Sports Illustrated*, and at the time of this writing is being considered as a future Olympic event. There are even MMA fantasy leagues. For example, *MMAplayground.com*, a website devoted to creating and managing fantasy leagues for MMA, gained nearly 10,000 subscribers within its first six months![3]

With its popularity increasing at an explosive rate, the bandwagon grows larger with the formation of other UFC-type groups like World Extreme Cagefighting, Pride Fighting Championships, Strikeforce, and Bodog Fighting, to name a few who wish to capitalize on this gold rush of a sport. Therefore, no matter what one's view is on the legitimacy of Mixed Marital Arts as sport, it has inarguably well-established itself in the life and hearts of many young Americans.

And since that is the case, when you ask young men what comes to their mind when they hear the word "fight" most of them will say one thing: MMA. Gone are the days when the dominant image of what constitutes fighting was two men donning boxing gloves for twelve rounds of jabs and uppercuts. Today, fighting signifies stepping into a cage and using a plethora of disciplines to force your opponent to signal his surrender by tapping out.

The Apostle Paul did not shy away from using athletic events as illustrations of the Christian journey. Indeed, even fighting was an acceptable biblical parallel (cf., 1 Cor. 9:26). Just as Paul describes, every Christian soon discovers that he is most definitely in a daily struggle with an all too familiar opponent. And it's not the devil and his demonic forces, or the great temptations of the fallen world, but our own indwelling sin. In the words of Walt Kelly, *"We have met the enemy and he is us."* And the struggle most definitely is a fight!

THE FIGHT WE ALL FACE

How many of you have bruises on your brow from banging your head against the wall in frustration due to the same sins pinning you to the mat again and again and again? Like me, do you ever get sick and tired of always going to Jesus and having to, with great exasperation, confess the same sin over and over, "Yes God, I did this again," thinking to yourself, "Surely the Lord has got to be as sick of this as I am." And because you cannot seem to defeat that particular sin, you find that your passion for spiritual things has waned, your sense of God's presence has been reduced to barely a blip on the radar and your overarching feeling is one of incredible, hopeless defeat. If you have never been in that position one of two things is true: either you're a brand new Christian or you are lying to yourself. Because to look at even the greatest saints is to see a picture of struggling with sin.

Take Paul. In addition to being called to apostleship by the Risen Lord Christ himself, Paul wrote more New Testament books than anyone else and was arguably the greatest church-planter Christianity has ever seen. No one in their right mind would question his spiritual vitality or maturity. On the contrary, most would hold him up as a model of what it is to follow Jesus. In fact, Paul was so confident of the work of the gospel in his life that he offered himself as a worthy example of a Christ follower. He told the church at Corinth, "Be imitators of me, as I am of Christ" (1 Cor. 11:1). No question, the Apostle Paul was one of the greatest Christians the world has ever known or will ever know.

Yet this same Paul also confessed in his letter to the Romans, "For I do not understand my own actions. For I do not do what I want, but I do the very thing I hate" (7:15). A few verses later, he continues to detail the struggle with sin:

For I do not do the good I want, but the evil I do not want is what I keep on doing. Now if I do

*what I do not want, it is no longer I who do it, but
sin that dwells within me.* (19-20)

Did you hear that? What does one of the greatest
followers of Jesus confess? *I know I'm supposed to do this,
but I find myself doing the opposite.* Writing those words
may have been very tough for Paul, but it actually gives me
encouragement. Reading a testimony like this helps me
come to grips with the fact that even the strongest and
most mature Christians among us find themselves in a
fight with indwelling sin! Indeed, followers of Jesus
struggling with sin has been endemic throughout history.

THE HEAVYWEIGHTS OF FIGHTING SIN

Examine the Puritans. These seventeenth-century men and
women knew what it was to fight sin. They wisely referred
to the struggle with sin as "The Long War." They
developed the idea of *mortification,* which emphasized the
daily process of killing (or mortifying) sin. Defeating this
evil opponent was a paramount to them: they talked about
it, preached about it, wrote books about it. You might see
them as the heavyweights of the sin-fighters!

Mortification was a well-embraced practice amongst
the Puritans because they knew how voracious an appetite
sin has –once it gets its teeth into a small part of your life,
it always aims for more. Like a hungry lion, it is
unrelenting until it has had its fill. Thus the Puritans spent
a lot of energy thinking about how they could best beat sin
into submission.

One of the better-known Puritan preachers was a man named John Owen. A seventeenth century English pastor, Owen wrote voluminously about the gospel and how one follows Christ. In 1656 he wrote *Of the Mortification of Sin in Believers*. Originally a series of messages intended to help Puritan teenagers in their fight against sin, Owen's work buoyed the hopes of Christians of any age as he shared the biblical strategies for defeating sin. Even today, great leaders of the church like J.I. Packer, John Piper, Sinclair Ferguson and C.J. Mahaney (to name a few) have looked to John Owen's work for both instruction and encouragement on how to best fight sin.

So let it be no surprise that in this book Owen will be someone I lean on heavily. Maybe it will help if we can see him as our fight trainer shouting words of guidance from our corner as we battle with indwelling sin in the cage of life. Owen not only was insightful into what the biblical text said about mortification, he also crafted memorable statements for Christians to reflect upon as they stand toe-to-toe with the sin which so easily besets them. For example, one of his more popular phrases truly highlights the stakes in our fight with this toughest of opponents:

Be killing sin or it will be killing you!

In other words, you are either going to work at tapping out sin, or sin will be tapping you out. Regardless of your choice, sin is already committed to work like crazy to make you submit. This reality forces us to reach one of two conclusions. Either we do nothing and lose, or we commit ourselves to fighting back in the hopes that our indwelling sin will continue to control less real estate in our hearts than when we first began the match! There is no middle ground. There is no equivocation. Like being on an icy slope, either you move your feet forward or you will find yourself going downward. To stop is to lose ground.

IT'S A FIGHT. BELIEVE IT.

This should cause us to embrace an obvious but critical truth as we look for ways to win our contest against sin: *you must believe it is a fight!* In order for us to take a strong step forward in defeating any sin in our life we must come to grips with the fact that we truly are in a contest against sin. Galatians 5:17 makes it clear:

> *For the desires of the flesh are against the Spirit, and the desires of the Spirit are against the flesh, for these are opposed to each other, to keep you from doing the things you want to do.*

If you are a Christian you have the Holy Spirit dwelling within to influence and lead you to a life that honors Christ and his Kingdom. At the same time you also continue to have sin residing in your fallen humanity, pulling you toward evil passions and God-dishonoring activities. The reality is you have a fight on your hands with an opponent who will leave you more than bloodied and bruised. Sin's desire is to sap your spiritual vitality, create static in your relationship with God and keep you on the mat of depression and despair as long as you will let it.

THREE RESPONSES TO SIN

Far too many followers of Jesus fail to realize they are in a real fight. In their words they may acknowledge the struggle with sin, but they rarely feel it in their innermost being. A heavy sobriety and brokenness over sin is absent from their customary experiences. Likewise, they lack a searing passion to conquer the very activities that hold them back. Usually, people take three different responses to sin in their life, particularly habitual sins which force them to tap out on a regular basis – discount, defeat or attack!

RESPONSE #1: DISCOUNT

The discounter knows he shouldn't do certain things but it's really not that big of a deal. Sin is viewed like a bothersome fly that harmlessly buzzes around. And because it is only bothersome but not dangerous, the person takes a "wink, wink" mentality to sin. People who hold this flippant perspective usually arrive there by compromising little by little over an extended period of time to the point that their heart is incredibly desensitized to sin. Unfortunately, unless the behavior in question is of the sort that would land you on the news or in jail, they don't see it as something to be too concerned about. Sin becomes discounted.

RESPONSE #2: SURRENDER

Others fight sin by simply waving a white flag. This is the person who has tried to battle a sin here and there but failed at it so miserably that they have given up. In other words, they've tapped out. Resigned to the idea that this sin will be a normal part of their life, often this person will seek to justify his chronic sinful practice by either appealing to cultural norms or simply reinterpreting the Scriptures to suit his liking. In reality, however, this person has already lost the fight. He hoists the white flag of surrender as he says, "This is just who I am, so it has to be okay."

RESPONSE #3 FIGHT

There is another type of person who enters the cage with sin. He is neither discounting sin's importance nor surrendering himself to sin's power, but instead he views the struggle with sin as a very real fight – a fight that is winnable! Possessing this perspective is critical to anyone making an effort to tap out sin.

THE VALUE OF SEEING THE STRUGGLE AS FIGHT

When an MMA fighter enters a match, he is fully aware that he must be adequately prepared at the moment he steps into the cage. There is no doubt the opponent will be seeking to do him harm. For that reason the fighter cannot afford to be passive. If he is to succeed, he must be ready to engage from the first moment to the last.

I have never witnessed a fighter respond to hearing the referee say "Fight" by raising his hand and saying to his opponent, "Hold on, I've got to finish this text on my phone." That would be ridiculous! Every fighter understands that failing to initiate probably means getting carried out on a stretcher. When it comes to a fight, hesitation equals defeat. That's why everyone is engaged mentally, physically and emotionally right from the word "Fight". That is what a fight demands! It is all the more true spiritually.

So what type of person are you when it comes to sin? Do you fight, wave your flag or discount it altogether? You must recognize that when you wake up sin is right next to you and has already had its morning jog. Embrace the fact that when you go to bed, sin will be up late in the kitchen planning tomorrow's attack. Puritan pastor John Preston wrote:

> *To profess to know much is easy; but to bring your affections into subjection, to wrestle with lusts, to cross your wills and yourselves, upon every occasion, this is hard.*"[4]

Fighting sin well takes work! Do you want to know how to defeat it? You begin by first seeing life "in the cage". In other words, you must believe it is a fight!

NEXT STEPS FOR A FUTURE FIGHTER

Some of us need to be reminded exactly how mean sin really is. We have forgotten that it plays for keeps and aims at nothing less than our complete and utter ruin. Let's go back to our fight coach John Owen. He bellows instructions from our corner, alerting us to sin's strategy to first delude you, then harden you, then ultimately destroy you. Owen writes:

27

Sin is always acting, always conceiving, always seducing and tempting...If, then, sin will be always acting, if we be not always mortifying, we are lost creatures.[5]

We must ask God to re-sensitize our hearts to any habitual sin that we have either justified or dismissed. Like David, we must cry out, "*Create in me a clean heart, O God, and renew a right spirit within me*" (Psalm 51:10). It would be wise for all of us to read Psalm 51 in its entirety, contemplating its soul-stirring expression of brokenness over sin and praying, "God, would you also do this work of grace in me?"

All Christians must arrive at one foundational conviction in order to win against sin: *you must believe it is a fight!* From the moment you wake up to the minute you lay down your head, you must recognize that you are in the cage with sin. When you begin to see that life not only is in the cage but life *is* the cage, you are well on your way to tapping out sin.

DISCUSSION QUESTIONS

1. Why is the Puritans characterization of the Christian's struggle with sin as "The Long War" an apt title?
2. How can we find encouragement in Paul's struggle with sin in Romans 7:15?
3. What does Owen's phrase, "Be killing sin or it will be killing you," say about the nature and aim of sin?

4. How is standing still spiritually a detriment to our walk with Christ? What can we do to move forward?

5. Which of the three responses to sin (Discount, Surrender, Fight) do you exhibit the most? How does that reveal what you really believe about sin?

6. In what ways does sin try to harm us?

7. What steps can you take to help see life as a *daily* fight with sin? Why is that perspective important in fighting sin?

2
BEFORE YOU ENTER THE CAGE

When I started, I used to go off just instincts.
Then they took head butts away,
so I had to learn some skills.

– MMA FIGHTER MARK COLEMAN

MMA fighters spend months in the gym preparing for a fight which could last mere seconds. This dedication to training is essential not only due to the physically grueling nature of the sport, but also because of the fighter's need to adequately defend against a variety of different fighting techniques such as grappling, boxing and martial arts. Those training to become MMA referees must be able to identify almost a hundred different submissions, transitions, sweeps, positions and takedowns.[6] You can bet the list will grow. Facing this diversity of attack necessitates an extremely intense and dedicated training regimen for the athlete.

Fighters-in-training focus on areas such as strength conditioning, strategic nutrition, technique improvement and mental focus. All of this is done in the hopes of increasing the fighter's speed, agility, power, flexibility, intensity, concentration and anaerobic capacity while trying to maintain body weight in order to hit the peak of their conditioning on the day of the match. This results in a thorough and committed process of weightlifting, dieting, sparring, running, watching videos and a host of other activities.

Fighters can take fairly extraordinary measures to ensure their "ring readiness". Some even tape their noses shut and wear snorkels during their workout, a technique known as hypoxia training, designed to build endurance by limiting the intake of oxygen. This unique practice is supposed to be the equivalent of high-altitude training, aiming to tutor the body into doing more with less oxygen. As a result, the body should ideally be more efficient at dealing with increased lactic acid in aching muscles throughout the fight, giving the fighter greater stamina and an edge to winning the match. So while it might look a little unorthodox, some commit to this unusual method believing it gives them the best chance at winning.

This introduces us to a very important maxim in seeking to tap out sin: what you do *out* of the cage is just as important as what you do *in* the cage. The actions and commitments you make before combating any sin in your life are just as critical as the actions and commitments you make in actual battle with that sin. So what "pre-fight" commitments must we make as followers of Jesus in order that we give ourselves the best chance of beating our most challenging habitual sins?

THE FIGHT IS A SPIRITUAL FIGHT

The work of mortifying sin is first and foremost a spiritual act. The only way to defeat any sin in your life is exclusively through the work of the Holy Spirit. The Apostle Paul, one of the all-time champion sin-fighters, noted in Romans 8:5-8:

> *For those who live according to the flesh set their minds on the things of the flesh, but those who live according to the Spirit set their minds on the things of the Spirit. For to set the mind on the flesh is death, but to set the mind on the Spirit is life and peace. For the mind that is set on the flesh is hostile to God, for it does not submit to God's law; indeed, it cannot. Those who are in the flesh cannot please God.*

This passage demonstrates that only people who live "according to the Spirit" will find the kind of victory God desires. The Holy Spirit is the critical agent in defeating sin. Listen to Paul in Ephesians 6:12:

> *For we do not wrestle against flesh and blood, but against the rulers, against the authorities, against the cosmic powers over this present darkness, against the spiritual forces of evil in the heavenly places.*

Pick whatever sin you struggle with – pornography, lack of courage, self-importance, pride, gossip – and at its baseline you will discover it ultimately is a spiritual issue.

This means you need spiritual resources to address it. Paul emphasizes that only those indwelt by God's Spirit can defeat sin in the manner God wants.

THE POWER OF THE HOLY SPIRIT

The Holy Spirit provides God's power to obey and serve him. Initially, the Spirit regenerates a person's heart, convicts them of sin and then grants them the power to live for Christ. When writing to the Corinthian believers about their conversion, Paul explains:

> *Do not be deceived: neither the sexually immoral, nor idolaters, nor adulterers, nor men who practice homosexuality, nor thieves, nor the greedy, nor drunkards, nor revilers, nor swindlers will inherit the kingdom of God. And such were some of you. But you were washed, you were sanctified, you were justified in the name of the Lord Jesus Christ and <u>by the Spirit of our God</u>.* (1 Corinthians 6:9b-11, emphasis added)

Here we clearly see that the Holy Spirit is actively involved in our spiritual growth, often evidenced by our departure from patterns of sin which held us captive in the past. His work in our life gives us power to conquer sin and increase our obedience. The well-known passage in Galatians 5:22-23 details the kind of "produce" that can blossom in our lives when we are led by God's Spirit:

> *But the fruit of the Spirit is love, joy, peace, patience, kindness, goodness, faithfulness, gentleness, self-control.*

DIAZ 5203

Available through **8/19/2020**

Don't forget to check me out!

33665030118203

It should go without saying that the role of the Holy Spirit is indispensable in fighting sin. Dependence upon his work is as much a non-negotiable as a fighter needing hands, feet and the ability to breathe. Owen writes, "A man may easier see without eyes, speak without a tongue, than truly mortify one sin without the spirit."[7] Unfortunately, we often enter the cage to face sin bereft of any real spiritual power.

BLIND & MUTE: SPIRIT-LESS FIGHTING

Those who do not have indwelling power of the Holy Spirit will attempt to overcome certain sinful practices by focusing solely on the sin itself. At first glance this strategy appears best. If I struggle with alcohol addiction, I need to stop drinking. If I'm hooked on internet pornography, then my efforts must be concentrated on staying away from the computer. The strategy is simple: *fix your sin by fixating on your sin.*

Unfortunately this turns out to be an incredibly threadbare and perilous way to fight. To address a specific sin without addressing the soul's lost condition is missing the forest because of the trees. It neglects the greater sin for the lesser. It is like merely bandaging a gunshot wound without attempting to remove the bullet which is fatally working its way to the heart.

Our greatest sin is that we are in rebellion to God. We seek our glory instead of his (Romans 1:18-22). That is the hellish bullet which must be dealt with first and foremost, and only the forceps of the work of Jesus at the Cross can bring adequate remedy. Dealing with our sin without the gospel is simply choosing to forgo the God-ordained life-saving instrument for a bandage than can only make our death look less messy.

When a person deals with their sin rather than dealing with the Savior, they are duped into believing that everything will be satisfactory once the hurtful behavior is gone. But removing a sinful practice from one's life isn't the same as removing our alienation from God. Only the gospel can do that. That is why merely fixing the problematic activity without addressing the entire soul is incredibly perilous. Not only does the person remain far from God, but he also gains a greater confidence in his performance.

Instead of growing in humility towards God who does for him what he cannot do for himself, he grows prouder in his self-efforts. Instead of glorifying God, he glories in himself. Instead of celebrating the grace of the gospel, he celebrates his willpower, intellect and moral aptitude in beating sin. However, as opposed to bettering his life, he ironically has made it all the more damnable. He now lives with greater false confidence in his ability to perform rather than realizing his need for divine rescue. The path that focuses on ridding people of individual sins outside of the work of Christ and the Holy Spirit may appear on the surface to offer real help, but in reality it only tenders further condemnation (cf., James 4:6).

OVERCOMING BAD ADVICE

Many believers' ongoing struggle with sin can be traced to the bad advice given to them by those who should know better – their pastors. There are ministers who pride themselves on being adept at giving "life application" sermons in the admirable hopes that even non-believers will not only be able to relate to what is taught but practice what is preached. Over the years I've heard pastors defend this approach saying, "*If the Bible is truth then it works no matter if the person believes in Jesus or not. Therefore, I want non-believers to practice the principles of the Bible to show it's true in the hopes they will be led to believe in the God of that Bible.*"

While the motivation behind that strategy is commendable, it weakly rests upon the principles of pragmatism. One could easily make the same case for the *Koran*, the *Book of Mormon* or other religious works outside the Christian Scriptures. They also would only need to proclaim, "This works so it must be true!" Since most of the world's religions have similar ethical and moral mores (e.g., love your wife, be kind to others, do good deeds), then I guess whoever can make their pragmatic case first to the unbeliever will be the one who wins.

Sadly, this approach tends to produce anemic sermons that revolve around thirty minutes of generalized moralisms and pithy truisms one could find in just about any faith or "Do It Yourself" talk show. When we fail to highlight the gospel and the congregation's need for Jesus, Sunday services can dangerously devolve into becoming about our performance rather than being overwhelmed by the One who has performed for us. Instead of hearing the gospel of grace, parishioners are given the Law, something which no one can keep well (cf., Rom. 3:23, 6:23).

This is the great and sad irony. Each and every Sunday, unbelievers come to church in hopes of learning about Jesus and his Good News. Yet after listening to one more "Try the Bible" message after another, they exit the sanctuary more fixed in their hellish trajectory than before they arrived that morning – all thanks to the church!

Again, while the evangelistic heart behind that philosophy is commendable, the practice of preaching aimed exclusively at behavior disconnected from the gospel can be very dangerous. The unconverted may very well find no reason to convert, thinking, "*Why do I need Jesus when I can make my life better through employing the principles of the Bible?*" Lamentably, the Bible becomes less about Good News and more about good advice with Jesus leading the way as Counselor, Life Coach and Self-Esteem Guru (or Revolutionary, Rebel and Countercultural Icon, depending on your flavor of Western Christianity) rather than Savior. Sermons revolve more around principles than a Person.

This lackluster preaching diminishes the mystery (and scandal) of the Cross, replacing it with steps, secrets and insights to enhance an already "you-centered" life. Pastor and author William Willimon rightly stated:

> *Who needs God when you've got simple principles? Such preaching has succeeded in doing what no preacher in the Bible – much less preacher Jesus – has ever done: reduce the vast, bubbling, mystery of biblical faith to slogans fit for a bumper sticker.*[8]

In the end, the lost are beckoned to perform, not repent. Jesus becomes simply another Oprah with "How To" tips and life enrichment insights. Thus Christianity – in the eyes of those seeking God – is seen as something you do, not something done for you through the Person and Work of Christ. Regrettably, without a clear connection to the gospel pastors run the risk of taking life-application messages and transforming them into death-ensuring messages that keep the lost confident in themselves but not a Savior.

They substitute a strategy of simply following steps in place of trusting in the Savior and depending on the work of his Spirit. As a result, many outside of Christ who attend church will continue to live under the false impression that the key to conquering any troublesome sin is to focus on that sin at the exclusion of the overall problem: a rebellious and depraved condition which can only be remedied by a Savior and replaced with a new life empowered by his Spirit.

THE NECESSITY OF FAITH IN CHRIST

In contrast, God's heart is that human beings address the entirety of their soul, not simply spotlighting one erroneous activity. Sin flows from a life that is spiritually dead. Without the life-changing work of the Spirit, it does not matter what bad habits and evil practices we discontinue in our lives, because our condemned status before God remains the same. Look at how Paul describes the spiritual state of mankind before conversion:

And you were dead in the trespasses and sins in which you once walked, following the course of this world, following the prince of the power of the air, the spirit that is now at work in the sons of disobedience— among whom we all once lived in the passions of our flesh, carrying out the desires of the body and the mind, and were by nature children of wrath, like the rest of mankind.
(Ephesians 2:1-3)

The picture painted is one of humanity's total depravity – sin has stained us through and through, leaving nothing untouched by its damning presence. To be "children of wrath" who follow the satanic leadership of the fallen world might not sound like the résumé we want, but it is nevertheless true.

Humanly speaking, we are irreparably broken (cf., Romans 3:9-18). Because that is our default state, none of us can remove our sin simply by sheer willpower or brilliant insight. The root of sin remains and will likely manifest itself somewhere else in life. You must address the entire soul by conversion, dealing with Christ before you deal with your sin.

In other words, a person must first become a follower of Jesus in order to successfully tap out sin, because only Christians have the Holy Spirit dwelling within them. Jesus said much the same when speaking to a man named Nicodemus about entering into the Kingdom of God:

> *That which is born of the flesh is flesh, and that which is born of the Spirit is spirit. Do not marvel that I said to you, 'You must be born again.'* (John 3:6-7)

We saw in the initial passage from Romans 8 that if we want to fight against the deeds of the flesh we must become people who *"set their minds on the things of the Spirit (v. 5)"*. Doing this will bring life and peace. We might say it brings us victory over sins in the cage. But in order to set your mind on the things of the Spirit you must first "live according to the Spirit" and that only happens when a person is born again through the work of the Spirit in the gospel of Jesus Christ. Simply put, you must become a Christian.

Jesus shared an apt metaphor with his disciples:

> *I am the vine; you are the branches. Whoever abides in me and I in him, he it is that bears much fruit, <u>for apart from me you can do nothing</u>.* (John 15:5, emphasis added)

Clearly, the first step to be taken in tapping out sin is to become a Follower of Jesus. It is to trust in who Christ is and the work he has done on our behalf at the Cross. Moving any further in our pursuit of fighting sin well without dealing with the gospel is akin to stepping into the ring without having done any preparation beforehand. Jesus warns that it is engaging the opponent without any real power, for apart from Christ we "can do nothing."

Stay away from that recipe for disaster and get right with the gospel before you enter the cage!

DISCUSSION QUESTIONS

1. Why is training such an essential part of fighting well?
2. What pre-fight commitments do you need to make in order to face sin in the cage at your peak?
3. Why are all struggles ultimately a spiritual issue? How does the role of the Holy Spirit intersect with your struggle with sin?
4. How would you define sin?
5. How can someone get into deeper trouble with sin by choosing to fight it outside the work of Jesus?
6. What is the difference between the Good News of Jesus and good advice? How does that fit with your understanding of the gospel?
7. How can churches potentially hurt sin-fighters in their quest to defeat sin?
8. Why is faith in Christ a necessity for beating sin?
9. How does a person become a Christian?

3
HOLDS THAT DON'T WORK

Ricky Bobby: *Hey, look, Frenchy, I thought about it. So why don't you go ahead and break my arm?*

Jean Girard: *I do not want to break your arm, Monsieur Bobby, but I am a man of my word.*

Ricky Bobby: *Here's the deal. He's not gonna break it because I'm gonna slip out of it right now. Houdini!*

– TALLADEGA NIGHTS

In an earlier chapter I noted sin – anything that misses the mark of God's heart and plan – is actively seeking to steal our spiritual strength, interfere with our relationship with God and pin us to the mat of despair. Indwelling sin easily proves to be one of the toughest opponents in the cage of life. Yet, in spite of sin's tenacity, believers in Jesus can take great hope in seeing victory over it in their lives.

THE HOPE WE HAVE

The Apostle Paul proclaims a foundational truth in Romans 8:13 when he writes, "For if you live according to the flesh you will die, but if by the Spirit you put to death the deeds of the body, you will live." This teaches that sin can be beaten, defeated, tapped out. It proves that when we engage our indwelling sin in the cage of life we can actually leave with more victories than losses.

A key aspect in this fight is found in the words "but if *by the Spirit* you put to death the deeds of the body, you will live." You know that one sin that always seems to have your number? The one that always leaves you flat on the mat? The Bible says that you cannot just fight it anyway you want, but instead it must done with the proper technique: "by the Spirit". In other words, even after coming to faith in Christ there is a certain spiritual approach we must take in order to truly tap out any one sin in our life. To do less is to live the life of a pretender instead of a contender.

I was reminded of this truth when I watched a MMA match between two equally dangerous fighters. Shortly into the match, one of the men had placed his opponent into what he perceived to be a great submission hold. A submission hold is grasping your opponent in such a fashion that he must quit ("tap out") or suffer great injury. These serious moves are match-clinchers. In fact, the majority of matches are won due to submissions rather than knockouts. So I'm watching this guy on top of his opponent in what he believes to be a good submission hold. He was so confident that he even started to get a little cocky – he would smile and nod his head like, "This match is all but over." All of a sudden his opponent, in one lightning-quick move, wrapped his legs around his opponent's head like a pair of scissors. He then slammed him to the ground while wriggling his hand free from the supposed "submission hold" and sent his no longer overconfident opponent into la-la-land via knockout.

Two thoughts popped into my head as I watched the turn of events. The first was, "Wow. I wish I could do that." The second was, "I guess confidence in the wrong submission hold can leave you submitting." Watch MMA fights for any amount of time, and it will not take long to conclude that sometimes fighters assume certain holds will work when in reality they may not work well at all. You can be in a fight thinking that you've got the upper hand and are moments away from winning, when in truth you are about to get pounded.

HOLDS THAT DON'T HELP

It's no different spiritually. There have been times in my life when I really thought I had beaten a certain sin into submission. I believed that performing "moves" X, Y and Z had created the perfect submission hold, forcing that specific sin to tap out of my life. But I ended up suffering a reversal of fortunes and saw that sin return with even greater vigor in my life. I was frustrated. I was despairing. The harder I tried, the worse and more frequently my sin harassed me. Somehow, the submission holds I had been employing in the cage against my sins only served to assist them in tapping me out time and time again!

How can you tell if you've got a good hold on your sin? Can you identify the difference between an authentic submission hold and another self-deception that provides opportunities for your habitual sin to land his match-ending move? How can we see if our activities are actually making progress toward defeating sin or simply giving the illusion of winning when in reality we are closer to defeat than ever?

To answer these questions, we must listen to the biblical insights on grappling with sin from John Owen, the Puritan pastor turned personal fight coach. Imagine Owen shouting out these instructions on the three signs of a bad submission hold as we grapple with our sin in the cage of life. Much of the remainder of this chapter has first passed through his hands.

1. A BAD HOLD LEADS YOU TO BELIEVE YOU HAVE KILLED SIN

Over the years I have watched many believers who have chronically struggled with one sin or another go to a Christian ministry or church that promised deliverance. Often the ministry's approach was something in the spirit of, "I'm going to say a prayer – name this and claim that – and when I am finished, you will never struggle with that sin again." In other words, these Christians were being led to believe that they were going to experience the ultimate submission hold on the sin that troubled them. They were to assume that when the ministry was finished with them, sin would not only be defeated but it will be dead, never to come back again.

Owen counsels against that type of hold because it promotes a perfectionism not found in the Bible. In fact, Paul says in Philippians 3:12, "Not that I have already obtained this or am already perfect, but I press on to make it my own, because Christ Jesus has made me his own." The apostle is saying, "I haven't arrived yet. I still struggle with sin. This is a life-long fight that I will continue to battle all my days." Unlike some denominations which appear to teach that Christians can reach some level of perfection in this life, the Bible (and the experience of every believer) demonstrates that none of us will be rid of sin utterly and completely until the return of Christ and the establishing of the new heavens and earth (cf., Rev. 21, Rom. 8:18-25).

Puritan pastor Richard Sibbes writes about the Christian and his continual struggle with sin,

> *The ground of this mixture is, that we carry about us a double principle, grace and nature. The end of it is especially to preserve us from those two dangerous rocks which our natures are prone to dash upon, security and pride; and to force us to pitch our rest on justification, not sanctification, which, besides imperfection, has some soil. Our spiritual fire is like our ordinary fire here below, that is, mixed; but fire is most pure in its own element above; so shall all our graces be when we are where we would be, in heaven, which is our proper element.*[9]

Sibbes points the reader to the truth that only in the glories of heaven – our "proper element" – will we cease to have sin as an opponent. Until then, the believer's life is "mixed" with sin. Our fight continues.

Submission holds promising the utter destruction of sin often set us up for greater failure. If we ever succumb to that sin following its supposed removal, we will be disappointed not only with ourselves but also with God, who was supposed to have already fixed us. We may despairingly begin to say, "You didn't come through for me, God. It is all your fault. I showed faith and you proved unfaithful!" As a result our faith starts to crumble, and we begin to fall into the downward spiral of spiritual depression – if not the complete abandonment of any semblance of a spiritual life with Jesus. All of this can be traced to a bad theology on fighting sin. If you believe that you can kill sin completely, you have a bad hold and setting yourself up for the life of a pretender. Good theology reminds us that we will never rid ourselves completely of sin while on this earth.

2. A BAD HOLD MERELY DIVERTS SIN

When I was in the process of buying my home, I noticed the air-conditioning unit was broken. During our initial inspection, I witnessed water gushing out of the overflow PVC pipe located underneath the ledge of the roof – a clear signal that something was wrong. We notified the owners about the needed repair, and a few days later they told us it was fixed. When we returned the repairs seemed complete, until I noticed the same water now flowing down the driveway. I walked around to the back of the house and saw they had simply attached additional PVC to the overflow pipe, allowing the water to travel along the rain gutters down the side of the house. Instead of stopping the water at its source, they had just diverted it to another part of the house. I was beside myself. We could not have cared less about where the water flowed to; we were more concerned about where the water was flowing from! Rather than repairing the problem, the owners had merely relocated it. What they believed was fixed was not fixed at all.

Often, what happens when people believe they have conquered a sin is that they have only diverted it. The water will continue to drip. It just drips in another area of the person's life. The truth is, sin does not merely affect us at the surface level (the end of the pipe) but begins at the root (the source of the flow). Consequently, we will never be repaired spiritually if our submission holds against sin only focus on stopping the surface sinful activity! The root of the sin feeding that specific manifestation will continue to flow no matter where you "move the pipe" in your life. Thus you may manage to stop one sinful activity, only to have another one of the same ilk surface in another area of life. In the end, all that supposed fighting of sin was actually diverting it instead of stopping it at its source.

A woman in my congregation once confessed to me that she deeply struggled with the sin of materialism, but felt like she had beaten it. When I asked her how she conquered it she said, "Well, I just don't go to the mall anymore." Initially I laughed, but she continued saying, "No, you don't understand. I used to go to the mall every weekend, and I would spend hundreds upon hundreds of

TAP

dollars because that was my god, my idol and something I just couldn't root out of my life, so I decided to stop going to the mall."

Later I saw her and asked how her strategy was working. She confessed it wasn't going so well. I asked if she had started going back to the mall. She replied, "No, I don't ever go to the mall. I shop online where I now spend thousands upon thousands of dollars each week." That woman was experiencing no victory over her sin; on the contrary, she was getting pinned to the mat with ease! She had simply "moved the water." Instead of dealing with the problem at its source she only relocated the manifestation of it. She had not dealt with her sin; she had only diverted it.

Here's another example. It is no secret that many men struggle with the sin of lust. Imagine that during your high school and college years you struggled with lust, becoming very promiscuous as a result. But over time you realized that sleeping around was not God's plan, and you decided to work very hard to stop that specific activity. In fact, you told yourself that when you got married your problem with lust would stop, because the bonds of marriage would be wonderful guardrails against promiscuous sex.

Consequently, you got married, and thankfully over the last twenty years you have been physically faithful to your spouse in marriage. But you have not been faithful mentally. The sin of lust you believed you had tapped out through marriage has resurfaced with a vengeance – as a two-decade addiction to pornography and continual fantasizing about people other than your spouse. Stopping promiscuity for pornography is simply moving the leak, diverting the sin. The root sin is still alive and well, ready to tap you out in a moment's notice. Nothing has really changed.

All sin-fighters must realize that even though one particular action ceased, another one can easily form because the source of sin that is feeding those actions was never addressed. That is merely diverting your sin, exchanging one manifestation of that one particular expression of sin for another. John Owen writes,

> *He that changes pride for worldliness, sensuality for Pharisaism, vanity in himself to the contempt of others, let him not think that he has mortified the sin that he seems to have left. He has changed his master, but is a servant still.*[10]

Pastor Tim Keller, using the idea of idolatry for the source sin, writes:

> *Dealing with the idols of the heart is an ongoing process. It is not "one and done"...we must always ask the "whys" and "reasons" behind our attitudes, actions and sin. What is the sin behind the sin? Too often I want to address only the symptoms at the neglect of the root cause.*[11]

Flee from any strategy for fighting sin that only combats it at the surface level. This is the practice of the pretender. Just because one dams up a polluted eastbound river, the water that now flows west remains putrid. It is still materialism for the woman; it is still lust for the man. They only sought to attack the "what" of their sin instead of first looking at the "why". As a result their lives were given to the soul-shrinking practice of moving pipes, continually dealing with the same water pouring out different sides.

Stopping a sinful activity does not necessarily mean we have conquered that sin and can rest with some sense of victory. In fact, we may be only moments away from being flipped on our back and put in a real submission hold by sin! Therefore, focusing solely on any one sinful activity at the exclusion of the source sin is a bad hold. By contrast, contenders work to discover the *sin behind the sin*. They look past the external action to the internal source feeding those actions.

3. A BAD HOLD ONLY GIVES OCCASIONAL CONQUESTS OVER SIN

What's the difference between a sleeping lion and a dead lion? Both are immobile, quiet and relatively safe – but at some point the sleeping lion will awaken and be very hungry. Sin is much the same. Unless it is soundly defeated, sin can make us feel like we have won simply by being quiet and still for a season, until it returns with a vengeance.

It is like a lion lying low in the tall grass waiting for the hunters to expend the rest of their ammunition, retire for the evening and lock their keys in the Range Rovers. Are those hunters still in danger while the lion is reposed?

Absolutely! But for a season it may appear that all is fine, even though there is a lion in their midst waiting for the right moment to pounce.

Many times we become proud of the submission holds we employ, thinking we have beaten sin, when in reality sin is merely waiting for the opportune time to strike. Like a lion in the tall grass, it may seem for a time that certain sins will not trouble us anymore. Having unloaded our ammo we conclude, with guns still smoking, that the lions must be gone. However, they may simply be waiting for the right time to wreak havoc in our heart – when we least expect it. We are misled, proclaiming victory in a field full of tall grass.

There are two common ways we think we have beaten sin, when all the while it lurks in a hiding place poised to pounce on us when the situation presents itself.

THE FALSE HOLD OF EMOTION

Sometimes emotions give us the illusion that sin has been defeated. We listen to a sermon, go on a retreat, send our kids to camp: we hear or see something that moves us so emotionally that we make these incredible resolutions to do this and stop that.

Take the perennial church camp experience for student ministries around the United States. Kids get away from their environments and plant themselves on a camp ground for a few days of preaching, singing, stories and other camp activities. It can be an emotional pressure cooker for some. At the end of the camp, countless decisions for God are made. How long do many of those decisions last? Maybe a month. Maybe not even a week. Or in the case of many adults, take a typical Sunday morning. You hear a message and are impacted emotionally, but that is as far as it goes. You are moved in your emotions but not your will. Privately you may make an intensely-felt decision to quit this sin or pick up this godly discipline – which quickly evaporates even before you sit down at the restaurant for lunch after church.

If only our emotions get stirred, it can give us the false impression that there are no lions in our midst. When we are emotionally pumped we feel as if nothing could stop us from following God. It is during these intense emotional times that sin likes to rest in the grass, waiting for this ephemeral season to pass so it can then get to the business of attacking and eating. Sin likely will not have to wait long, because emotion has an incredibly brief shelf-life. That is why you have many people make all kinds of decisions for God at camps, retreats and getaways only to have them return to their sinful ways weeks (if not days) later.

Emotion makes a great side dish but fails horribly as an entrée. You cannot live off that diet for very long and find success in the ring against sin, because it can give you the sense you are winning when you are moments away from disaster. Again.

THE FALSE HOLD OF BUSYNESS

When I was growing up in West Texas, I heard a student pastor tell his young men if they ever struggled with lust to go outside and do something physical (since this was, in his opinion, a predominantly physical problem). He would counsel them to run laps, hit the weight room, or just go outside and chop wood. In fact, that became his phrase: "If you struggle with lust – go chop wood," an especially funny concept in the largely treeless West Texas prairie. The idea behind this approach is that the person will not engage in sinning as long as his mind is distracted. But the problem is that you can only chop wood for so long. At some point either you run out of wood, or you have to go home. At some point you have to stop running laps. At some point you have to put the dumbbells down. At some point you have to go back to your house, your school, your work. You eventually must re-enter your regular world where the hungry lion is waiting for you. Busyness tries to pass itself off as the spiritual discipline of preoccupation. Preoccupation only dabbles on the surface of things and never strikes at the root. It merely distracts us from the reality that there is a lion in the grass waiting for things to calm down, giving us no incentive to go after him with guns blazing.

When we have occasional victories over sin, it may mean we are just "chopping wood" and "running laps" or simply worked up emotionally – all those practices lose steam quickly. Whichever disappointing avenue we take, in the end we will be right back at square one with our sin. The sin that has our number will continue to control us. There have been many times in my own life where I believed I had a great submission hold on sin. It was going to tap out in my life. But nothing happened. On the contrary, I was fighting sin using powerless holds, ineffective holds that sin could reverse on me with ease. There must be a better way!

DISCUSSION QUESTIONS

1. How can believers find hope in their struggle with sin from Romans 8:13, "For if you live according to the flesh you will die, but if by the Spirit you put to death the deeds of the body, you will live."?

2. What are some examples in your life that lead you to believe your strategy for fighting sin may be ineffective?

3. How would you respond to a Christian who says they are on their way to completely eradicating sin from their life?

4. How would you counsel someone who boasts that his sin can never harass him again?

5. What does it mean to divert sin as opposed to defeating sin? What ways have you simply diverted a sin instead of defeating it?

6. What does it mean to have a *sin behind the sin*? How can we get to the root sin in our life?

7. How can emotion and busyness offer us a false sense of tapping out sin? What are other things that can give us a false sense of beating sin?

4
HAVING A GOOD HOLD

I'm going to fight a guy who is way bigger than I [sic]
but it doesn't matter to me because skill beats size.
Technique beats strength all the time.

– UFC WELTERWEIGHT CHAMPION
GEORGES ST. PIERRE

The Gogoplata, Can Opener, Guillotine, Kimura and Flying Arm Bar – what do these terms have in common? No, they are not the latest punk bands you might hear on the radio. They are the names of different types of MMA submission holds. It seems there are as many submission holds as there are creative titles. All of them have one thing in common: if you can get your opponent into one of these holds, it usually forces him to surrender by tapping out.

The most common submission hold, the *arm bar*, is a grappling hold that hyper-flexes the elbow joint by using the body's full leverage on the opponent. Correct execution of this move almost always assures the fighter of victory in the cage.

Wouldn't it be nice if there were similarly effective submission holds for the Christian's fight against indwelling sin – holds that actually worked? What would they look like?

As discussed in the previous chapter, poor holds can lead Christians to think they have completely eradicated sin, when actually they are experiencing only occasional conquests over sin or simply diverting it to another area of their life. They are unable to keep sin pinned to the mat. What if, instead of using holds that allow us the pretend victory of temporary success, we discover a spiritual arm bar in our battle with sin? Our fight coach, John Owen, highlights three characteristics of a good submission hold, enabling genuine progress toward the defeat of indwelling sin.

A GOOD HOLD HABITUALLY WEAKENS SIN

Think of a MMA fight that goes to the final round. Who usually leaves the ring the victor? The fighter whose consistent attacks weaken his opponent after each round – his punches becoming less precise, his kicks becoming less powerful, all his movements slower and more predictable – is on the road to victory. The same is true in fighting sin. You can be confident that you have a good hold on the sin you struggle with when its power to tempt you becomes weaker and weaker over time.

Reflect on a sin you have chronically grappled with over time. How easily does that sin's attack affect you? Do you see its power to tempt you growing stronger or weaker in your daily battle? Is your resolve to move forward in the face of that sin being reinforced or undermined with each assault? If you are fighting sin well, you will notice the waning of temptation to that particular sin and begin to see it increasingly tap out throughout your life. This does not mean that any sin will evaporate or vanish forever, but it does mean that you can win against it – and win frequently!

Some Christians who have been constantly beaten by "pet" sins over the years might argue this cannot happen, but it is clearly possible. Sin's fighting power can diminish over time. In an earlier chapter, we read of the Apostle Paul's ongoing struggle with sin (Rom. 7), but he also penned these words within the same text:

> *We know that our old self was crucified with him in order that the body of sin might be brought to nothing, so that <u>we would no longer be enslaved to sin</u>.* (Romans 6:6, emphasis added)

That is an incredibly powerful statement! Because of the gospel, because of what God has done for us through Jesus Christ, we can actually win over sin! Sin does not need to have the upper hand. On the contrary, believers in Jesus Christ have been given, in him, the ability to effectively deal with sin. Galatians 5:24 says, "And those who belong to Christ Jesus have crucified the flesh with its passions and desires." This is a very graphic statement (much more graphic than anything you would witness in a MMA fight)!

The violence inherent in the crucifixion paints a clear picture of the power available to followers of Jesus who want to tap out sin. You can actually put a sin that has your number in a submission hold whereby its power to tempt you diminishes until it is essentially dead. That is what crucifixion is – nailing somebody through his hands and feet upon a cross until they are weakened enough to the point of death. Paul's graphic imagery demonstrates that through the power of the Gospel, sin's hold on you can get weaker and weaker and weaker to the point of no longer seriously troubling you. In a practical sense, you are "dead" to it.

We will delve more into this glorious truth in a later chapter. However, I cannot describe how hopeful understanding this critical truth is for followers of Jesus who have struggled with sins that have owned them for far too long. Amazingly enough, the sin that has your number does not have to have your number anymore. There is a way to win against sin.

Many Christians have become far too comfortable with the false idea that struggling with habitual sins must be par for the course. They acquiesce to the idea that no matter how aggressively you fight sin, you must accept that seasons of winning will be matched with seasons of defeat. In this frustrating cycle of fighting sin, the believer never comes to a place of outright victory. Fortunately, this does not have to be the case for any Christian. While sin will always be present in this life, constantly seeking to thwart our walk with God, we can actually tap out certain sins with great amounts of regularity. But to achieve victory, your submission hold must result in the habitual weakening of sin.

A GOOD HOLD CONSTANTLY CONTENDS WITH SIN

Some think that great saints are those who rarely speak of their struggle with sin. Preachers often refer to sin in such light and even flippant ways that their congregants conclude, "Man, our pastor never talks about sin or his struggle with it; on the contrary, all he ever preaches about is victory, dominion, destiny and success. He must be incredibly strong and spiritually mature!" I would argue this thinking is misled.

In fact, I believe that great saints are those who are acutely aware of their sin. They never rest or quit training in their fight against it. Throughout my ministry I have repeatedly seen a maxim at work: people in periods of great spiritual growth usually have a greater awareness of their sinfulness.

I spoke with a friend who was experiencing exponential spiritual growth in his life. After he shared with me all the wonderful things God was doing in his life, he expressed a genuine concern that had been growing in his heart: "It seems the more I grow, the more I realize how far I have to go. The more personal holiness increases in my life, the more sin I see. I am having more areas of my life in need of sanctification flash before my eyes. It is like I am seeing more sin in my life than ever before!"

Fortunately, he wasn't in a bad place at all. In fact, he was spiritually "in the zone", walking with Jesus in the presence and power of the Holy Spirit. One of the main roles of the Holy Spirit is to convict the heart of sin (cf., Jn. 16:8-11). Consequently, if the Holy Spirit is greatly working in someone's life, it is natural (or supernatural) for the person to possess an acute awareness of sin. This should not be a cause for alarm but rather encouragement, because God is showing the believer how much more of his life can be leveraged for the glory of God. Those who are open to the convicting work of the Holy Spirit can see areas of our lives in need of sanctification that other believers may ignore due to lukewarm complacency. My friend's situation was not a curse but a blessing – a gift from God.

People who find victory over sin are those who know it is going to be a tough, daily battle. They never stop fighting! They never accept the idea that one sin or another must always pester them for the rest of their days. Great saints wake up every day swinging and kicking, knowing that sin is ready to finish them off before they even leave the house.

You can tell the difference between a *contender* and a *pretender* in how they go about their day. One lets sin strike at him uncontested, while the other is vigilant to hurt sin in as many ways as he can. The Christian who is adept at tapping out sin in the cage of life has grown deaf to the ring of the closing bell. He is always fighting. John Owen notes, "Such a one never thinks his lust dead because it is quiet, but labors still to give it new wounds, new blows every day."[12] It is a mistake to think mature Christians never struggle with sin; the truth is that we cannot grow well spiritually unless we are fighting some sin or another.

Furthermore, to contend with sin is to strive to understand your opponent. When an MMA fighter gets in the cage with his competition, he brings not only his moves but also his mind. Most fighters would say that mental preparedness is more critical than physical readiness. A good fighter has done the homework on his opponent. He knows his methods, his strengths and weaknesses, what types of punches he likes to throw, which part of the ring he likes to work, etc. He studies these details because to understand your opponent is to know better how to defeat him. An inferior understanding of your opponent's tendencies puts you at a great disadvantage when you fight in the cage.

Good submission holds on sin are based on a thorough understanding of that particular sin's line of attack. How well do you know the strategy that your sin uses? If pornography is the sin that habitually defeats you, ask yourself – does that sin usually tempt you when you are alone for an extended period of time? Does it amplify its attack when you have not gotten enough rest? If materialism is your pet sin – does it strike when you come across some extra money? Do you find it increases the assault when you compare notes with the Joneses?

The reality is that your sin knows you. It probably knows you better than you know yourself. Part of sin's strategy is to go after your weaknesses and leverage them against you, so that it can arm bar you into submission. Therefore, if you want to successfully fight against sin, you must know what scenarios put you in a vulnerable position. You need to think through the potentially dangerous places in life which leave you open for sin to quickly tap you out. Knowing your weaknesses and how a particular sin can exploit them is simply doing your homework on your opponent. Then, when it makes its move, you can deflect its attack, set up a counter attack of your own or hopefully not even be around that part of the ring in the first place! Understanding the tendencies of a certain sin is part of fighting that sin so that every hour of every day, you know where to best strike. A good hold constantly fights and contends with sin.

A GOOD HOLD FINDS FREQUENT SUCCESS

Doesn't this make sense? If you are fighting a certain sin using the same strategies and submission holds but repeatedly find yourself tapping out at the end, it would appear that those strategies and holds are ineffective. Prudence (and your natural aversion to getting bruised and bloodied) would dictate that you change your strategies and learn new and better submission holds, ones that work and do not let you down when fighting in the ring. Changing from ineffective holds that you have mastered to new holds – even if they take some time to learn – is anything but crazy. On the contrary, it is the only way to avoid a losing record against your opponent that increases every time you face off.

You have probably heard the well-known statement that insanity is doing the same thing over and over expecting different results. Unfortunately, when it comes to combating sin in our life, many pick the insane road by never adjusting in the cage. For some reason, many believers have in their mind that if they just stick to their current strategy of fighting sin – if they just pray harder, listen to more sermons or memorize enough Scripture – they will one day conquer their struggle with lust, jealousy, covetousness or whatever habitual sin has chronically bloodied and bruised them over the years. Their minimal experiences of victory ought to be enough to show them that their current submission holds are supremely ineffective.

In the end, these battered Christians can easily feel that they have let God down – or worse, that God has not fulfilled his end of the bargain. But to remain committed to a flawed strategy is to walk a crazed and sorrow-filled path. Believers must instead take a lesson from the world of MMA (and most any sport): if your opponent is beating you, then you must adjust your strategy.

You can trust that you are on the road to defeating sin when you notice a growing number of notches in your win column. Good submission holds win and win often. But what does success against sin look like? Coach Owen puts it this way:

> *[Success is when sin's] motions and actions are fewer and weaker than formerly, so that they are not able to hinder his duty nor interrupt his peace—when he can, in a quiet, sedate frame of spirit, find out and fight against sin, and have success against it.*[13]

Owen is not saying the specific sin you struggle against is gone forevermore (see Chapter 3), but when it does attack you find yourself quickly and conclusively rejecting its temptation. Furthermore, you proceed throughout your day aware of but unhindered by that temptation. In other words, a good submission hold doesn't allow a specific sin to have your number anymore. It may continue to cross your path in order to tempt you, yet the pull of that temptation grows weaker with every attempted strike. You discover that its continual blows and kicks are easier to absorb, deflect or counter. You are winning. This is the path of the contender. This is the way to tap out sin.

ARE YOU EXCITED OR DISCOURAGED?

My hope is that our knowledge of effective and ineffective submission holds will reveal to each of us where we are in our fight against sin. Maybe this has helped wake some of us from the slumber of thinking we were doing well, when in reality we are just a move or two away from being beaten...again. Others may be relieved knowing that not only has God not failed them, but there really is hope for beating sin. Still others, bruised and beaten after years upon years of losing in the cage to a specific sin, still think it is too good to be true.

No matter where you may find yourself, there is likely one question remaining. Now that we have seen the characteristics of both good and bad submission holds on sin, what is the technique for an effective attack? What is "the move" to be made which results in winning? What is to be done in order for us to find more victories than defeat? How can we tap out sin? For that, we must keep reading.

DISCUSSION QUESTIONS

1. Why is a good sign of conquering sin the *habitual* weakening of that sin?

2. How does Galatians 5:25, "And those who belong to Christ Jesus have crucified the flesh with its passions and desires," inform us of the gospel's power against sin?

3. Why is it easy for Christians to become comfortable with the fact that certain sins will continually plague them for the rest of their lives?

4. Do you agree or disagree with this statement? *Great saints are those who are acutely aware of their sin.* Why?

5. How would you encourage someone who told you that the more they have grown spiritually, the more sin they see in their life?

6. Why is it important to understand how particular sins fight against you? How can you discover any sin's "plan of attack" in your life?

7. How can you tell when you are actually winning the battle against a certain sin?

8. How can a small group of committed Christians help you get a good "submission hold" on your sin?

5
REPENTING OF REPENTING

Just 'cause you feel it doesn't mean it's there.

– RADIOHEAD, *THERE THERE*

Kevin Ferguson is a name you might not know. This Bahamian-American who resides in Miami made his name through fighting, but not the MMA variety. Ferguson's expertise was street fighting. He would throw punches with anyone, anywhere – in an alley, in front of a warehouse, anywhere he could find a taker. With his cronies filming the bloody contests and then uploading them to the Internet, Ferguson soon became an underground sensation. Most knew him by his nickname: Kimbo Slice. As fight after fight filled up computer screens across America, Slice's popularity continued to grow. Rolling Stone even dubbed him "The King of the Web Brawlers".

The increasing attention prompted Slice to up the ante with his fighting "career". He entered the world of MMA much to the chagrin of many of the ring's veterans. They wondered if the untrained street puncher could be successful in a sport built upon the foundation of not only strength and quickness, but also discipline, technique and strategy. It did not take very long for the truth to surface. By the fourth match in his very early career, Kevin Ferguson, a.k.a. Kimbo Slice, was exposed.

After beginning 3-0 (a record often discounted due to the poor quality of his opponents), Slice found himself scheduled in a match with a UFC Hall of Famer named Ken Shamrock. Even though Shamrock was forty-four years old at the time and arguably past his prime, many believed that Shamrock would teach Slice a lesson about how authentic MMA athletes fight in the cage. Sadly, Shamrock never got that chance. He suffered a cut in training on the morning of the match, and doctors would not clear him for the fight.

At the last minute, another fighter was substituted on the debut card with Slice that would be shown on CBS Sports that evening. The fighter's name was Seth Petruzelli, who had been scheduled to fight Aaron Rosa in the light heavyweight portion of the undercard. This had the makings of another easy win for Slice in a relatively uncompetitive match – not to mention the fact that the contest was hosted in Slice's backyard, the BankAtlantic Center in Sunrise, Florida.

However, nothing could have been further from the truth. While Petruzelli gave up thirty pounds to the heavier Slice, he was a much more accomplished MMA fighter. His background spoke volumes about his commitment to fighting technique and discipline. Petruzelli was a full-contact karate champion and wrestling star at Cape Coral-

Mariner High. He said of Slice, "Before I even knew I was fighting Kimbo, I'd see him on the Internet. I didn't like his style. I hate the street thing. I'm more of a technique type of guy. I've been in martial arts my whole life and I just thought he was some thug."[14] Even with his background, he did not fight full time. At the time of the match, Petruzelli was running a Smoothie King in Orlando. He was an MMA fighter – but one on the fringes of the profession.

When he arrived at the BankAtlantic Center, he was expecting to be in a non-televised undercard contest. His intent was to fight the match and then return to his day job doling out fruit drinks. Instead Petruzelli was offered the chance to fight the famous (or infamous) Kimbo Slice on national television. He accepted the offer and tangled with Slice in front of a live audience of 7,732 fans and many more via the tube. The match was scheduled for three five-minute rounds. It only took 14 seconds.

Within moments of the referee's call to fight, Petruzelli knocked Slice out with one well-placed punch to the chin. For Kimbo Slice it was over – both the match itself and his reputation as a legitimate MMA fighter. The national media denounced Slice as a fraud, just as those inside the MMA circles had asserted all along. Instead of being a contender, Kevin Ferguson was a pretender. In facing Petruzelli, he highlighted for the world an important truth about fighting: proper technique is critical to success. The Petruzelli/Slice match clearly testified that a person can be heavier, stronger and faster than his opponent, but without proper technique he nearly always will wind up tapping out or simply being exposed as a fraud.

You must have the right technique to win. If you don't care about form but simply want to trade blows with an experienced fighter, you will only reveal to everyone that you are a pretender rather than a contender. You may believe you are good at fighting, but like Kimbo Slice (at least early in his young career) you are just fooling yourself. It will only be a matter of time until you are exposed.

HAVING THE RIGHT TECHNIQUE

How many followers of Jesus expose themselves as pretenders when it comes to battling with indwelling sin? At one time or another, all of us have approached a certain sin in our life with confidence in the soundness of our attack strategy only to wind up on the mat, succumbing to its soul-punishing temptations in our actions and thoughts. We have been exposed – assuming ourselves to be contenders when we are truly impotent in our ability to defeat any specific sin. Instead of holding our arms high in victory, we are carried out of the ring in defeat over and over again. This outcome should prompt us to realize that we must develop a proper fighting technique lest we live the illusory and ever-disappointing life of the pretender.

How can we fight sin well and not fool ourselves? How can we demonstrate that we are contenders when it comes to fighting our sin? One of the ways we do that is by discovering what kind of repentance we employ in our fight against sin.

Repentance is the *sine qua non* of spiritual growth – an essential part of the whole. Far from being only an isolated action which leads to the door of faith in salvation (cf. 2 Cor. 7:10), repentance also makes up the room in which Christians dwell. Martin Luther penned in the first of his "Ninety-Five Theses" these words: "Our Lord and Master Jesus Christ...willed the entire life of believers to be one of repentance." Pastor and author Tim Keller concurs:

> *Repentance is the way we make progress in the Christian life. Indeed, pervasive, all-of-life-repentance is the best sign that we are growing deeply and rapidly into the character of Jesus.*[15]

This demands that we get repentance right in our contest with sin. Therefore, as we battle sin we must ask a key question: Do we repent well? We may have more losses than wins concerning certain sins in our life due to the fact that we repent poorly. This chapter will examine elements of false repentance in the hopes that we can avoid being exposed in the future as pretenders.

REPENTANCE GONE WRONG

There is a way to demonstrate false repentance that conflicts with the biblical pattern and – instead of contrition – actually displays our pride and self-interest. Consider the example of the nation of Israel in Psalm 78:32-35:

> *In spite of all this, they still sinned;*
> *despite his wonders, they did not believe.*

73

> *So he made their days vanish like a breath,*
> *and their years in terror.*
> *When he killed them, they sought him;*
> *they repented and sought God earnestly.*
> *They remembered that God was their rock,*
> *the Most High God their redeemer.*

Israel clearly experienced a severe discipline at the hands of the Lord. This judgment obviously produced a very unhappy situation for God's people, driving them to seek God in repentance. They earnestly repented, remembered and sought the Lord. Sounds good, right? Surely this repenting would rectify their familial relationship with God. But notice how God views their repentance as the psalm continues:

> *But they flattered him with their mouths;*
> *they lied to him with their tongues.*
> *Their heart was not steadfast toward him;*
> *they were not faithful to his covenant.*
> (78:36-37)

Here we see the DNA of imitation repentance: words without heart. Israel's repentance was insincere. They told God that they were sorry for their wrongdoing, but he knew that their hearts were still committed to their sins. Israel's subsequent actions revealed that truth. Shortly afterwards they were exposed as pretenders, those same sins demonstrating their unfaithfulness to his covenant. Instead of real brokenness over their iniquities, God's people feigned repentance to obtain rescue from the consequences of their sins, but not the sins themselves. As such, God did not recognize their repentance – because pretender repentance is not repentance at all.

Israel's example should help us see that sometimes the greatest hurdle to fighting sin is our very repentance of it. Listen to Paul's encouragement to the church at Corinth:

> *As it is, I rejoice, not because you were grieved, but because you were grieved into repenting. For you felt a godly grief, so that you suffered no loss through us. For godly grief produces a repentance that leads to salvation without regret, whereas worldly grief produces death.* (1 Corinthians 7:9-10)

Pretender repentance is a dead end. If we demonstrate anything but godly grief over sin, we will not win many matches against it. What tragic irony – the very instrument which should bring Christians into deeper relationship with God and embolden their attempts at tapping out sin actually keeps their hearts far from God and chronically pinned down by sin. Therefore, if we would fight sin well, some of us may actually need to repent of how we have repented in the past.

REPENTANCE MISDEFINED

The world for repentance in Greek (*metanoia*) is literally translated "to change one's mind." Unfortunately, the literalness of that definition has led many a teacher to conclude that repentance is simply agreeing with God about your sin. Thus, to repent, all a person need do is acknowledge through prayer, "God, I agree that _____ is sin. I shouldn't do it," and move on, confident that God has forgiven them. However, this definition of repentance is inadequate, leaving us with the understanding that repenting is nothing more than giving words to the obvious.

I believe the motivation behind this instruction is likely born from a heart seeking to fully trust in the finished work of Christ as the penalty of our sins. However, it can regrettably produce a one-dimensional, sterile and even mechanical response whereby a sinner simply affirms with God that the said activity is wrong, maybe even verbalizes some kind of regret and continues on with their life.

However well-intentioned that counsel may be, I believe it has helped foster counterfeit repentance in many a Christian. I know it did for me. For years I understood repenting of sin to be almost a formulaic process: I sin, immediately confess that sin to God then proceed with my life telling myself that to feel any sense of loss or grief was simply a lack of faith in the gospel. "God forgives, Yancey," I would think, "Get over it and have some faith in the complete work of the Cross!"

While I do believe Christians can unnecessarily wallow in grief over sin (exposing a weak confidence in the gospel), which was not my case. Sadly, over time I crafted a very self-styled repentance founded in a selfish attempt to make myself feel good about continuing in sins that had plagued me for years. I was not repenting for God; I was repenting for me. I was trying to hide my sins with the gospel instead of letting the gospel attack them. As a result, my chronic sin issues were exposed on a regular basis, because mine was the repentance of a pretender.

PRETENDER REPENTANCE MAKES GOD A MEANS TO AN END

My pretender repentance was not motivated by grief over sin and its vileness but solely by a desire to avoid suffering the consequences of sin. For example, a Christian struggling with a certain sin attempts to repent because he is tired of feeling shame, frustration or disappointment. His failure to obey is bothersome and gives him a "downer" of a day, so he repents with the hope of moving on with life, without ever experiencing any real remorse or brokenness over that particular sin.

Needless to say, this is not true repentance that "leads to life" (Ac. 11:18) but the kind of repentance evidenced by Israel in Psalm 78. The act of repenting can itself be sinful when done with a heart seeking only to alleviate personal discomfort at the expense of a real relationship with God. In essence, what we have is a believer who wants what God gives but does not want God himself. John Owen describes the heart of this person when he writes: "They want to be healed unto themselves but not unto God."[16]

Jonathan Edwards, another Puritan pastor, exposed the pretender heart when he wrote, "As the love and joy of hypocrites are all from the source of self-love, so it is with their other affections, *their sorrow for sin*, their humiliation and submission, their religious desires and zeal."[17] Pretender repentance makes God a means for selfish ends.

The unfortunate result is a pattern of repentance evidenced by an emotionless, robotic "confession" with the individual continuing on his way as if nothing ever happened. Ironically, while the pretender believes he has acted in faith to deal with his sin, the stark reality is that because of his self-styled, relationally-disconnected, man-centered repentance, his particular "confessed" sin has now been imbued with greater strength. Like an inoculation, the pretender experiences just enough elements of repentance (e.g., acknowledgment of sin, asking for forgiveness) to keep him from experiencing the genuine article. Consequently, he will most likely find little victory over any sin; on the contrary, his life will probably be marked by frustration and even despair as he finds himself easily submitting to those same sins over and over.

PRETENDER REPENTANCE DOES NOT LAST

Another way that pretender repentance evidences itself is how quickly a person re-engages the sin of which he has repented. For example, I would easily slip back into sins I had repented of only days if not hours before. It eventually dawned on me that only agreeing with God about my sin was insufficient. It also did not seem to matter how frequently I said I was sorry.

Indeed, I had told God that I was sorry so many times that I began to feel less sorrow for that particular sin as time went on. Instead of having a soft heart toward sin, my shallow repentance was actually hardening my heart –

callusing it further and further to the sin of which I was attempting to repent. In the end, though I was repenting often I was not growing through that repentance. On this path I was not going to tap out troublesome sin any more than I was going to sprout wings and take to the air.

PRETENDER REPENTANCE FOCUSES ON THE WRONG CRITERIA

Pretender repentance evaluates its effectiveness by different criteria than real repentance. Since this shoddy repentance really never helps the fighter vanquish sin, one must look to other markers to feel any sense of accomplishment. For example, I have heard many teach that we repent well when we find ourselves quickly confessing our sin as soon as we have disobeyed.

Now, while I do believe immediate repentance is a good thing, the evaluation of our contrition should not revolve around how much time elapses between your sin and confession but on how much less that person actually commits that sin in the future. Do not measure the authenticity of repentance with a stopwatch but with obedience. Is the better fighter the one who repeatedly raises himself up off the mat after being laid out ten times a round (thinking he is winning in the process), or is it the one who is pinning sin to the mat ten times each and every round? The answer is obvious. Christians will only evaluate their repentance by something other than obedience if the repentance they exhibit is pretender's repentance. For far too long I assumed my repentance was both real and effective. Regrettably, it was neither.

CONCLUSION

What does your repentance look like? Do you find any of these characteristics of pretender repentance in your life? Do you need to repent of your repenting? If so, it probably is a big factor as to why you find yourself being defeated by sin so often in the ring. So how does real repentance evidence itself in the life of a sin fighter? In the next chapter we will look at the characteristics of the repentance of a contender.

DISCUSSION QUESTIONS

1. Why is repentance essential in fighting sin?
2. What does Martin Luther mean when he says, for the Christian, *all of life is repentance*?
3. What is your definition of repentance? How do most people understand repentance?
4. How can repentance devolve into merely a formulaic process? How does that affect our heart to God? What can we do to keep us from that kind of repentance?
5. What does it mean to make God a means to an end instead of being an end unto himself? How does false repentance contribute to making God merely a means?
6. In what ways does pretender repentance hurt our future ability to repent well?
7. What does this statement mean: *You don't measure the authenticity of repentance with a stopwatch but with obedience.*
8. How can we repent of any pretender repentance?

6
CONTENDER REPENTANCE

Repentance is a heartfelt sorrow for sin,
a renouncing of it, and a sincere commitment
to forsake it and walk in obedience to Christ.

– WAYNE GRUDEM, *SYSTEMATIC THEOLOGY*

L ooking at biblical portrayals of repentance brings to light a stark contrast to the distant, matter-of-fact repentance of the pretender. Consider King David's words in Psalm 51:1-12, which many consider the *textus classicus* of biblical repentance:

> Have mercy on me, O God,
>   according to your steadfast love;
> according to your abundant mercy
>   blot out my transgressions.
> Wash me thoroughly from my iniquity,
>   and cleanse me from my sin!
> For I know my transgressions,
>   and my sin is ever before me.

Against you, you only, have I sinned
  and done what is evil in your sight,
so that you may be justified in your words
  and blameless in your judgment.
Behold, I was brought forth in iniquity,
  and in sin did my mother conceive me.
Behold, you delight in truth in the inward being,
  and you teach me wisdom in the secret heart.
Purge me with hyssop, and I shall be clean;
  wash me, and I shall be whiter than snow.
Let me hear joy and gladness;
  let the bones that you have broken rejoice.
Hide your face from my sins,
  and blot out all my iniquities.
Create in me a clean heart, O God,
  and renew a right spirit within me.
Cast me not away from your presence,
  and take not your Holy Spirit from me.
Restore to me the joy of your salvation,
  and uphold me with a willing spirit.

Read it again (maybe even aloud). Do not try to break it down verse by verse but absorb it in its entirety. Does David's plea to God in light of his sin with Bathsheba sound like mere agreement? Granted, this is a psalm, which likely means it was put together with much contemplation and artistry, but juxtapose the heart of this confession with the shallow repentance many evangelical Christians tend to emulate.

David felt led to pen an entire Psalm centered on his repentance, showing us that real, biblical repentance should at least be more than merely, "I'm sorry, God," then moving on as if nothing has transpired in our relationship with the Most High God. That is Psalm 78 pretender repentance, not Psalm 51 contender repentance. The repentance we see in David is a sorrow of the soul, a brokenness of the spirit and a deep desire for God to restore that which has been strained and spent by sin. David's repentance is authentic. Again, it is contender repentance, which is uniquely evidenced by those who desire to tap out sin in their lives.

Let me be clear here. I do not think we must write a psalm in order to demonstrate biblical repentance, but our heart should be affected in such fashion that it brings with it a substantive difference in our future actions. When Jesus told the Pharisees in Matthew 3:8 to "bear fruit in keeping with repentance," he shows us that repentance must actually carry with it a real change of life. Far from just agreeing with God about your sin, there should be an evident alteration in your life from sinful behavior to obedient behavior. Examining Psalm 51 helps us observe further indicators of what true, contender repentance looks like.

CONTENDER REPENTANCE REMEMBERS IT'S ABOUT A RELATIONSHIP WITH GOD

David's repentance reveals what is at the heart of sincere repentance: a deep, abiding sense of a relationship with God. David cries in v. 4, "Against you, you only, have I sinned and done what is evil in your sight." This is not about David and his sin as much as it is about David and his God.

Sin, first and foremost, is an offense against the Creator. Theologian Wayne Grudem defines sin as "any failure to conform to the moral law of God in act, attitude or nature."[18] Sin, by definition then, is an action that has weightiness precisely because of how that action, and the person who commits it, intersects with God's command and character. Therefore, when we sin, our first strike is not against others or even ourselves but directly against a holy God. Knowing that your sin is primarily an assault on your relationship with God is the ground of good contender repentance.

David's grief and subsequent repentance flowed not from his desire for an easier, guilt-free life, but from his walk with the Lord God. That foundational truth oozes from his closing words: "Cast me not away from your presence, and take not your Holy Spirit from me. Restore to me the joy of your salvation, and uphold me with a willing spirit" (vv. 11-12). Contender repentance first focuses on the strain that sin brings to our relationship with God before it seeks to deal with any brokenness in other areas of our life.

Conversely, pretender repentance ignores the relational aspect of sin. For instance, in the past I would express sorrow over my sins not so much to repair my familial relationship with God but to feel psychologically free from any sense of guilt. My repentance flowed more from convenience than conviction. In my immature mind, my bare-bones apology had fulfilled my obligation to God and allowed me to get on with my life.

When we settle for this false repentance, we reveal a mistake in how we view God. We want to relate to God as Judge but not as Father. We are only sorry for the consequences of sin instead of seeing how it affects God's heart. Timothy Keller rightly calls out this pretender repentance with great insight: "That is not repentance, but rather self-pity. You will only avoid the sin in the future if it hurts you; the sin itself has not become ugly to you and it has not lost its attractive power over you."[19] How true! As we noted in the previous chapter, while I desired God's gift of forgiveness, I did not desire God. Unfortunately, this inept, self-centered strategy of dealing with sin never leaves anyone consistently victorious in the cage of life.

CONTENDER REPENTANCE DESIRES TO HATE SIN

As strange as it may sound, the path to developing a foundation for good, biblical repentance is hatred: namely, a hatred for sin. Puritan Thomas Watson said, "Christ is never loved till sin be loathed."[20] If we are to make any headway in tapping out specific sins we must cultivate hatred in our hearts. Because pretender repentance often wallows in the mud of self-indulgent ease, people can find themselves cheaply repenting of a sin but knowing they will soon willingly reengage it.

Like the aforementioned Israelites of Psalm 78, he finds peace in giving God empty words while his heart is filled to the brim with the desire to return to that exact same sin. The Puritans saw this poor sin-fighting technique in their day as well. Matthew Mead notes, "Many do, by their sins, as mariners do by their goods – cast them out in a storm, wishing for them again in a calm."[21]

In hating sin we are attempting to mirror God's heart. Proverbs 8:13 says, "The fear of the LORD is hatred of evil." Listen to how Psalm 97:10a extols those who believe, "O you who love the LORD, hate evil!" What you hate clearly reveals what you love. Detesting evil demonstrates love for God. In fact, our hatred for sin reflects, unquestionably to a much lesser degree, how deeply and infinitely God hates sin.

When the prophet Isaiah saw the Lord in his glory he immediately cried out, "Woe is me! For I am lost; for I am a man of unclean lips, and I dwell in the midst of a people of unclean lips; for my eyes have seen the King, the LORD of hosts," having clearly recognized his own sinfulness and God's absolute distinction from it (Isa. 6:5). Similarly, when the writer of Hebrews paints a picture of the character of Jesus, he underscores Christ's abhorrence of wrongdoing: "You have loved righteousness and hated wickedness" (1:9). Hating sin is merely modeling God's response to sin and demonstrating your heart's fidelity to follow Jesus.

One of the ways you can cultivate a hatred for sin is to reflect on how greatly your transgression costs. Not only has sin brought strife, war, envy, greed, lust and every imaginable evil into creation and our hearts, but it also led to the crucifixion of Jesus on our behalf. That should be incredibly humbling. When it comes to the great work of the gospel, I am reminded that the only thing I bring to the Table of Redemption is my iniquity. My sin cost Christ his life. Reflecting on that sobering truth should invigorate my hatred of sin. 1 Peter 1:17-19 reads:

> *And if you call on him as Father who judges impartially according to each one's deeds, conduct yourselves with fear throughout the time of your exile, knowing that you were ransomed from the futile ways inherited from your forefathers, not with perishable things such as silver or gold, but with the precious blood of Christ, like that of a lamb without blemish or spot.*

Peter encourages the churches of Asia Minor to live a holy life with the clear knowledge that they have been ransomed from their sins by the most costly of gifts – "the precious blood of Christ." Reflecting on that truth brings a helpful sobriety and weightiness to even the most seemingly trivial sins. Jesus took lashes on his back for our angry tongue. His beard was ripped out of his face because of our penchant for gossip. He had nine-inch nails driven through each of his wrists due to our inability to keep our eyes from wandering.

Frankly, his death alone – aside from its violence or gore – should be enough to further embolden our faith against the temptation to sin. However, the horrific nature of his death gives the mind much more to meditate upon when attempting to cultivate a hatred for sin. It beckons us to see the Cross relationally and not just doctrinally, where at times we can easily distance ourselves from the gravity of our sin. When we work to increase our loathing of sin, it demonstrates in some small way our attempts to come to grips with the enormity of the sacrifice made by Jesus in order to accomplish our redemption.

Our resolve to exhibit real repentance increases when our loathing for sin does the same. Hating sin helps incline our hearts to respond with true brokenness over sin. It also forms an integral part of the fountain from which other godly emotions flow – sorrow, grief, humility, etc – emotions we see beautifully cascading down Psalm 51. Conversely, growing our hatred of sin will replace the flippancy found in much of today's quick, self-serving repentance with genuine, soul-wrought grief from a heart that has been nurtured on seeing sin as it truly is.

CONTENDER REPENTANCE SEEKS TO RID ALL SIN

When a Christian hates his sin he will seek to rid himself of all of it, not just some of it. This is an important component of repenting well. This is not a quest for perfectionism, a teaching found in some Protestant traditions, but an earnestness of heart which desires to abandon any and every sin with which it struggles. Contenders seek to repent of all their iniquities, not solely asking God to forgive them of one particular sin while secretly harboring others. Pretender repentance wants to rid itself of only that which bothers his peace, well-being or convenience while willfully and steadfastly clinging to other sins which are just as destructive. "Coach" John Owen describes this false repentance:

> *Whoever speaks peace to himself upon any one account, and at the same time has another evil of no less importance lying upon his spirit, about which he has had no dealing with God, that man cries 'Peace' when there is none.* [22]

In other words, if one comes to Christ to repent over one sin yet knowingly holds onto other iniquities of which he has no intentions of repenting from, then that person is engaging in false repentance and will receive no genuine peace in his life from God.

Contender repentance differs in that it looks for all sins from which to turn. Thomas Watson adds to Owen's thoughts:

> *A true convert seeks the destruction of every lust. He knows how dangerous it is to entertain any one sin. He that hides one rebel in his house is a traitor to the Crown, and he that indulges one sin is a traitorous hypocrite.*[23]

Watson gives strong language to prove a very serious point: contenders come before God with both hands held open before them instead of offering one sin in repentance while furtively clinging to another sin behind our back. Contender repentance seeks to rid itself of all known sin.

CONTENDER REPENTANCE WAITS FOR GOD'S PEACE

I am sure all of us at one time or another have sinned and quickly prayed to God, "I'm sorry," while proceeding with life as if nothing ever happened. Maybe you offer God a big sigh, shake your head, and tell him, "I should not have done that Lord. My fault," then merrily move on with your day. While we cannot know the heart behind someone else's response, I do not think it would be too radical to suggest that those types of actions frequently fall short of contender repentance. Instead, as we noted earlier, those prayers actually become our inept attempt to manufacture a feeling of peace, making God a means to an end. Again, this hasty repentance is the practice of the pretender. Unfortunately, although pretenders think their shallow repentance has ameliorated their relationship with God, it actually does the opposite.

Think of it this way. You discover that a very close friend has been spreading lies about you, so you invite him to dinner to discuss this hurtful situation. As you both sit down to eat, you, understandably hurt by his actions, share with him how lying is not only wrong but how it has affected you. Upon hearing you passionately state your case, your friend replies with little to no emotion, "I agree. That was wrong. I'm sorry," then continues to eat as if nothing ever happened.

Would you consider that genuine contrition? Of course not! In a genuine relationship, one person's sin against the other has not only broken a law, but the relationship has taken a hit as well. A quick, easy "repentance" would be rightly interpreted as flippant, inauthentic and incredibly selfish. The offender's motives are exposed: just wanting to move on, not really reconcile. The lack of brokenness speaks volumes about the real heart behind the apology.

If that is true in our relationships with each other, imagine how much more true it is of our walk with God! In Jesus we are not only given God himself but "a friend who sticks closer than a brother" (Prov. 18:24). The gospel gives us a proximity to God that we never could have achieved for ourselves. In fact, before Christ we were infinitely removed from God. Ephesians 2:1-3 says:

And you were dead in the trespasses and sins in which you once walked, following the course of this world, following the prince of the power of the air, the spirit that is now at work in the sons of disobedience— among whom we all once lived in the passions of our flesh, carrying out the desires of the body and the mind, and were by nature children of wrath, like the rest of mankind.

Notice how Jesus' work at the Cross redefined our relationship with God. From birth we were far from God, but in Christ, we have been reconciled to him. Paul continues in Ephesians 2:13, "But now in Christ Jesus you who once were far off have been brought near by the blood of Christ." 1 John 3:1 echoes this refrain when it reads, "See what kind of love the Father has given to us, that we should be called children of God; and so we are." No longer are we spiritual outcasts destined for God's just wrath, but now we have become God's beloved children, received and adopted into his holy family (Gal. 4:5, Eph. 1:5). The work of Jesus at the Cross gives us a closeness with God unparalleled by any earthly relationship.

It is this intensely-connected relationship with God that often is forgotten when we seek to repent from any sin. Consider the sting of a friend's false contrition – how much more does God our Father feel the pain of our pretender repentance? Quick, sterile apologies never cut it with God. John Owen refers to this type of pretender repentance as "speaking peace to your sin lightly," noting Jeremiah 6:14 which reads, "They have healed the wound of my people lightly, saying, 'Peace, peace,' when there is no peace." God sees right through this type of inadequate and mechanical repentance.

Whenever we sin we must understand that it is first and foremost a relational matter. King David highlights this aspect of our walk with God when he writes in Psalm 66:18, "If I had cherished iniquity in my heart, the Lord would not have listened." Sin creates relational static with God. Does he love us in Christ? Yes. Does he forgive us in Christ? Yes. Does our sin then still affect our walk with him? Yes. Like a friend who spreads lies about you, the need for relational reconciliation demands a genuine response of contrition. While it is true that the gospel keeps us tied to God no matter our performance, the brokenness we display over sin should reflect our relational closeness with Jesus.

However, because many want to feel good about their pretender repentance, it is not unusual for them to seek solace in the words of others like family, friends or even pastors. They share their struggle and how they have asked God for forgiveness, hoping that in return those people will reassure them they are on the right path and can experience peace. Similar to the flippant prayer of confession to God, trying to get others to make us feel better about our pretender repentance is another way we manufacture a false peace about our sin.

Often the people we have spoken with may have the same shallow definition of repentance. They hear the story of our succumbing to temptation and ask, "Did you confess your sin to God?" If we have, they simply reply, "Well then, move on and forget about it," never seeking to get beyond the words to the heart behind them. Unfortunately, they may have chosen to put pleasing men over pleasing God.

But what if your friend counseled you differently? What if he said, "Do you have a great sorrow in your heart about your sin? Have you seen the sin in light of the cost of the Cross?" Or what if he replied, "Maybe God wants you stay wounded relationally for some time because you appear to not really have taken it to the Cross."? I believe this can be sound counsel for some because it leaves the feeling of peace as something only God can bestow. Contender repentance understands this truth: only God can grant peace. You cannot manufacture it through cheap repentance or the opinions of other believers. It only comes from God.

CONTENDER REPENTANCE IS A GRACE FROM GOD

Puritan pastor Thomas Watson defines repentance as "a grace of God's Spirit whereby a sinner is inwardly humbled and visibly reformed."[24] If one is to have genuine contender repentance, it must be given to him by God. Only the work of God's Spirit on the heart can produce the fruit of real repentance. Scripture is replete with that testimony.

> Acts 5:38, *"God exalted him at his right hand as Leader and Savior, to give repentance to Israel and forgiveness of sins."*

> Acts 11:18b, *"Then to the Gentiles also God has granted repentance that leads to life."*

> 2 Timothy 2:25b-26, *"God may perhaps grant them repentance leading to a knowledge of the truth, and they may come to their senses and escape from the snare of the devil, after being captured by him to do his will."*

Is repentance something I do or something God does in me? The answer to that question is "Yes." This is the mysterious economy of God in repentance – it is a work of God's grace as much as it is something we do. For that very reason I believe it is wise counsel that anyone who desires to fight sin well should spend time in prayer asking God to grant him this most precious and effective resource in tapping out sin. Ask God for contender repentance.

DISCUSSION QUESTIONS

1. In what ways does David's prayer in Psalm 51 mirror real repentance?

2. What did Jesus mean in Matthew 3:8, "bear fruit in keeping with repentance"? What does that fruit look like?

3. How does having a real relationship with God affect our repentance?

4. How can repentance be about our convenience instead of real conviction over sin?

5. What does Thomas Watson mean by this statement: *Christ is never loved till sin be loathed*. Why is hatred of sin necessary for fighting it effectively?

6. Why does fighting well include a heart which seeks to rid itself of every kind of sin, not just the "big sins"?

7. How can thinking of sins purely as "big" and "small" hurt our struggle to repent well?

8. What does it mean to wait for God's peace in repentance? How can we wait well?

9. If real repentance is a grace from God, what does that teach us about God, his sovereign power and our fight against sin?

7
TAPPING OUT SIN

It's one thing for sin to live in us;
it is another for us to live in sin.

– JOHN MURRAY

Throughout this book we have attempted to better understand how Followers of Jesus can find victory over the sins which so easily beset them. Victory comes more readily to those who begin by seeing their lives as happening "in the ring." Every morning they awake prepared for a real fight with sin. We have examined what constitutes success (and failure) when it comes to battling our sins with various "submission holds," evaluating ourselves as either contenders or pretenders. The intent up to this point has been to gain a clearer picture of authentic victory over sin, as opposed to just living under the illusion of victory. Hopefully the progression of chapters has led us to ask the most important question: *How do we defeat sin?* What is the key to tapping it out? What do we need to do in order to rack up more wins than losses against this toughest of opponents? That's what I will address in this chapter.

To tap out sin we must begin with *belief before behavior*. This is absolutely fundamental for victory! In fact, this entire book has been written in such a way that each chapter ultimately leads to that one truth. Winning over sin – experiencing lasting victory in the cage of life – will only come when we focus on belief before behavior.

FIGHT THE ROOT OF SIN WITH BELIEF

If you are a follower of Jesus, the first thing you need to understand is your status regarding sin since you became a Christian. When you crossed the line of faith, you entered into a completely new reality described by the Apostle Paul in Romans 6:

> *We know that our old self was crucified with him in order that the body of sin might be brought to nothing, so that we would no longer be enslaved to sin. For one who has died has been set free from sin...So you also must consider yourselves dead to sin and alive to God in Christ Jesus.* (6-7, 11)

This is a huge passage for those who struggle with sin – which of course means all of us! This section of Scripture details our spiritual status prior to becoming Followers of Jesus. Our life before Christ was "enslaved to sin". That is a big truth to grasp. Before we were converted, our lives were at the mercy of sin – it was our master. Sin had dominion over us. Whatever it beckoned us to do, we did.

But something changed when you became a Christian. Romans 6 goes on to say that upon embracing the gospel of Christ we have "been set free from sin". Let me reiterate that once more: the Bible teaches that those who have given their life to Christ and his work at the Cross have been liberated from sin!

Now surely someone will ask at this point: *in what way have we been set free from sin?* Paul's words cannot mean that Jesus' work at the Cross has freed us from the presence of sin. Our own experience tells us sin is still with us. So from what has the work of the Cross freed us? Two things: the gospel sets believers free from the *penalty* of sin and the *power* of sin. It frees us from sin's penalty in that we will not receive God's just wrath at the end of the age, otherwise known as hell.

The gospel also liberates believers in Christ from the power of sin. Sin does not have to be our master anymore. It does not have dominion over us. In the past we did sin's bidding no matter what, but as a follower of Jesus, sin does not own us anymore. Thus, we do not have to sin. We have been freed from sin's power. This is the Gospel's beautiful work in us through Christ, of which the great hymn *Rock of Ages* proclaims:

> *Be of sin the double cure,*
> *cleanse me from its guilt and power.*[25]

That is why the gospel is so critically important in trying to tap out sin. Christ's work on the Cross is not only significant for those who are looking for Jesus but also for those who have found and are trying to follow him. In his wonderful book *The Discipline of Grace*, Jerry Bridges illustrates how many believers think the Christian life should be lived following our conversion.

From this diagram[26], we see that the unbeliever needs to receive the work of Jesus on the Cross (i.e., the gospel), but after you become a Christian what you need most are the spiritual disciplines of discipleship – that is, you need to do things in order to grow in holiness. This was the track I was given. I became a Christian at ten years old. Before that time people (e.g., parents, pastors and friends) told me what I needed most was the gospel. Then upon receiving Christ and becoming a believer I was told I now needed to do things for God in order to grow spiritually.

How was I to do that? I was told I needed to "*do the disciplines.*" Immediately I was instructed to begin practices such as reading the Bible, praying, and serving. Now, before I am accused of going somewhere that I am not, let me answer a question that may arise in some readers. Are the spiritual disciplines bad? Not at all, in fact I think they are good things. Indeed, they are critical to fighting sin and growing in Christ! There is, however, something that should precede them and give them their rightful context: the gospel.

What we need most *before* coming to Christ is the gospel. What we need most *after* coming to Christ is the gospel!

Why is the gospel important after becoming a Christian and how does that impact the practice of spiritual disciplines? If Romans 6 teaches us that at the Cross Jesus freed us from the penalty and power of sin, it means we have not been defeated by sin! On the contrary, the gospel makes it possible for us to win against any sin we face. Did you catch that? Think about that one sin which owns you – the one to which you easily and repeatedly submit. The gospel says that not only do you not have to listen to its soul-shrinking temptations but that you can actually beat it. You can tap it out more often than it does you! That is the glorious work of the gospel when it comes to fighting our toughest of opponents. It is the essential belief we must have in the forefront of our mind as we enter the cage to fight sin.

The significance of the gospel compels us to employ a critical strategy for fighting sin. Defeating sin is not first about doing things but believing truths – belief before behavior. We *must* grasp this! Without it we will not have any lasting victory over the sins that pin us to the mat. We must believe and trust in what God has done through Jesus at the Cross before we attempt any behavior to try to grow in holiness. For all who desire to tap out sin well, it is necessary to begin with the "double cure" of the gospel. The key is belief before behavior.

THE TRAP OF PERFORMANCE

When our spiritual disciplines develop independent of the fertile ground of the gospel, we can easily fall into the trap of performance. Those who live the Christian life on the performance track believe that victory or defeat concerning sin is totally dependent on their abilities and effort – it is all up to their execution in the ring. They may say things like *I know I can beat this habitual sin if I just study the Bible enough. If I just pray harder I will find real victory! If I just involve myself in more ministries then I'll win over sin.* This is life on the performance track.

Do you realize how tough this is? Now the pressure is really on, because victory or defeat entirely rests on what you bring into the ring. Unfortunately, this is how many Christians view their fight against sin. While they might give voice to a different theology, in all practicality they believe that after God saves them, living the Christian life is all up to them.

Sadly, this performance-based fighting can easily lead people into a new legalism. Believers degenerate into attempting to earn God's favor, thus leaving them with two possible outcomes. Some will likely become self-righteous, complimenting themselves on their own holiness and maturity based on how much they have accomplished spiritually. This successful person proudly points to spiritual activities like Bible study, prayer, or serving in ministry to indicate their maturity and the reason they win over sin.

Alternately, others may fall into despair, mourning their failure, because even after vigorously engaging in the same spiritual activities listed above, they cannot seem to really win against certain sins. Ironically, two people can do the exact same disciplines and both be completely ruined spiritually – one by pride, the other by hopelessness.

Does your spiritual life typify one of these two results? Do you find yourself filled with pride in your own spiritual activity? Or are you depressed because you feel unable to do enough to experience victory? Some may live vacillating between the two. If you find yourself in one of these scenarios, you may need to embrace the truth that combating sin begins with belief before behavior. Fight your sin with gospel first.

HOW THE GOSPEL DEALS WITH SIN

There are many reasons why the gospel is so powerful in dealing with those sins we struggle greatly against. Let me mention two.

1. THE GOSPEL DEALS WITH THE GUILT OF OUR SIN

When I write of guilt I do not mean a person's sense of feeling bad about something they have done. Frankly, we are guilty whether we feel emotion about our transgression or not. If you drive Mach 5 through a school zone and a police officer pulls you over, he likely will not care how you feel. He will, however, issue you a ticket because you are guilty. You have a legal guilt. It is the same with God. He has established his law in the universe, and when we break it, regardless of how we feel, we are guilty. We have a moral and legal guilt before a holy God that must be dealt with justly. However, the Bible tells us that the Cross takes care of our sin guilt.

Second Corinthians 5:21 says, "For our sake [God] made [Christ] to be sin who knew no sin, so that in him we might become the righteousness of God." When you set your faith at work on Christ and take your sin before the Cross, you are reminding yourself that the eternal penalty of that sin which so easily taps you out has already been taken care of in the gospel. Think about that most amazing of realities! Jesus bore the brunt of the Father's just wrath in our place on the Cross for every sin we have committed in the past, are committing in the present and will commit in the future – and gave us his righteousness in return.

Pretty good news, is it not? All of those sins you struggle with, all that junk you cannot overcome, all those iniquities that knock you around in the cage: God took all of it and put it on the Cross! And he did this to such an extent Paul says it is as if Jesus became sin for us. Why? So that when God places his justice on his Son, we get Christ's perfect obedience placed upon us. That means when God looks upon you He sees Jesus' perfect righteousness – it has been reckoned to you by the work of the Cross.

Now, I am confident the details will be somewhat different, but let me paint a scenario for you. One day

every believer will die and stand before God on his
judgment seat at the end of the age, and he will examine
our lives and everything we have done – the darkest acts
and most shameful thoughts included. God will look at us
who have been clothed with Christ's perfect obedience and
say, "I find no fault in you." Didn't I say this is good
news? Because of the gospel, we "become the
righteousness of God" (2 Cor. 5:21). That is why Paul,
under the full inspiration of the Holy Spirit, can
confidently proclaim in Romans 8:1, "There is therefore
now no condemnation for those who are in Christ Jesus."

Some need to draw a circle around the words "no
condemnation" as an act of faith. Sadly, that may be
difficult to do if you have been running on the
performance track and have been defeated by certain sins
which cause you to feel great shame and guilt. You are
missing the glory of the gospel. *What if I mess up a lot?*
No condemnation. *What if I'm still addicted?* No
condemnation. *What if I still get tapped out?* No
condemnation for those who are in Christ Jesus – we have
been saved by grace!

When I am battling a sin, it is that gospel-
encouragement I need to hear. It starts with belief not
behavior. I need to take my sin that I cannot seem to shake
free of and take it to the Cross, crying out to God:

> *Lord, I can't beat this thing. And I know how
> horrible it is in your eyes and that your justice
> needs to deal with it. That's why I'm here at the
> Cross because I'm reminded that Jesus has taken*

care of my sin for me; he's taken away the guilt of pornography, materialism, envy, fear (whatever sin you are dealing with). He's taken the guilt of it and freed me from its penalty.

So I want to remind my own heart by dwelling upon the gospel that you have made right what I cannot make right. In Christ, you have done for me what I cannot do for myself. In Christ, I'm forgiven! I'm loved! I'm accepted! Because of that gift of salvation, I want to come before you and your great gospel in faith...

This is where you exhale! Unfortunately, some have forgotten what it is like to exhale because they have run on the rails of performance for so long. Fighting sin in particular (and living the Christian life in general) becomes all about us instead of all about Christ. The hopeless legacy of performance is an oppressive, spirit-shrinking faith not really worth having. Sadly, it is a legacy that often leads people farther away from Jesus and the grace-filled life found only in him.

This is why the gospel is critical as the context of spiritual disciplines. Its message of grace derails us from the tracks of performance-based, spirit-oppressive faith. The gospel strikes at the pride of the self-righteous by declaring that our right standing with God and all other blessings procured for us by Christ at the Cross have nothing to do with how well we know the Bible or how many hours we pray. They come to us solely and utterly by God's unmerited favor. The gospel simultaneously encourages the despairing as well, by assuring them that even though they haven't performed well, Christ has performed well for them. Hebrews 10:14 says, "For by a single offering he has perfected for all time those who are being sanctified." No matter how poorly I fight sin, I know the contest has ultimately and finally been decided. Jesus clothed me with his perfect righteousness – now and forever! In the gospel, God does for us what we cannot do for ourselves. It is why our fight against sin begins with the gospel before anything else – belief before behavior.

2. THE GOSPEL CREATES GRATEFUL LOVE IN OUR HEART

Knowing we not only have been freed from sin's guilt but also from sin's grip should make us incredibly grateful. We are grateful that we do not have to merit God's love, acceptance or forgiveness, because Jesus has already achieved that for us in the Cross. In Christ, God pulled us out of the sea when were drowning, and that greatest of rescues should produce in our hearts a wonderfully profound gratitude and love for God.

Grateful love for Jesus and his work on our behalf is the only fuel that can effectually power the engine of the spiritual disciplines. Reflecting on the goodness and greatness of God's grace in the gospel changes the motivation of the heart. Now, I serve, pray and read the Bible not because I am trying to climb the spiritual ladder of performance to earn God's favor in my life, but in response to my growing sense of love and gratitude for

Christ and what he has done for me. Understanding this gospel-centered motivation is essential to tapping out sin!

At the risk of sounding overly simplistic, ultimately, the reason we commit any sin is because in that moment we love that particular sin more than we love Christ. This is true for sins big and small. The reverse is also true for obedience. We obey in a specific situation because we love Jesus more than sin. This does not mean you can't obey the commands of God's Word without love for God. You can. It just won't be the obedience God desires. He desires for us to obey him from the heart. Our obedience must flow from our love (cf., Mt. 22:37).

This also means that in order for us to defeat any sin in the ring of life we must fill up our heart so greatly with love for God that it will overpower and replace the love we have for whatever sin that seeks to defeat us. Puritan Thomas Chalmers said, "The only way to dispossess [the heart] of an old affection is by the expulsive power of a new one."[27] Strong sins can't be merely removed, they must be replaced – a lesser love with a greater love.

So how can we stoke the fires of our love for God? How can we increase our affection in that it overwhelms lesser loves? By continually feasting upon, having commerce with and mediating upon the grace we find in the gospel! John Owen calls us to the same when he writes, "Let faith look on Christ in the gospel as he is set forth dying and crucified for us."[28] This is the best means to growing a grateful love in us, which can dispossess the heart of the most entrenched of sins.

The question then becomes *how can we continually feast on, have commerce with and mediate upon the grace we find in the gospel?* The spiritual disciplines! We use practices like prayer and the study of Scripture to continually refocus our heart's attention to God's grace to us in the Cross. In doing so a grateful love grows for Jesus in response to his grace, while "lesser loves" of sin have decreasing less space in our heart. We will have a "heart...strengthened by grace" (Heb. 13:9). By using the spiritual disciplines to consistently keep us at the foot of the Cross, we fight love with love! As we let the gospel stoke the fires of grateful love in our hearts, we not only let belief precede behavior but also allow it to inform, direct and enliven that behavior. This is how we fight sin well.

HOW ARE YOU USING SPIRITUAL DISCIPLINES?

While spiritual disciplines are good, and even essential, for fighting sin, they can also be deadly. Remember, practices like Bible study and prayer are spiritually damaging when perceived as ways to merit more of God's love and favor. Instead of being means *of* grace, they are viewed as means *to* grace. But the gospel tells us we are already completely loved and fully accepted by God. No amount of praying, serving or reading the Bible can change that. That is the beauty and wonder of the gospel of grace. It gives traction to our spiritual growth because it empowers us through the Spirit in our responsibilities to holy living while simultaneously forgiving us when we don't live up to those responsibilities.

That's why spiritual disciplines shouldn't be a burden to us. On the contrary, as we use them to further dine on the goodness of the gospel of grace, they should reaffirm to us that our burden has been lifted (cf., Mt. 11:28-30). If I'm feeling guilty because I missed a "Quiet Time" one morning, then I've also missed something else: the very reason I was doing devotional times to begin with! Disciplines, used properly, should confirm in our hearts the wonderful grace we have received in the gift of Jesus Christ.

Christian disciplines are bread not barter.[29] They are the way we feast upon God's gracious rescue of us in Christ. Practicing them well doesn't gain us more love *from* God, but allows us to increase our love *for* God! They are to be pathways to the foot of the Cross, where God's love for us is fully displayed – pathways we are to walk again and again as we re-experience the joy and wonder of God's great salvation of sinners.

To see them as anything less (or more) is to fall prey to the dead-end path of spiritual stagnation. We should heed the counsel of Paul to the Galatians, "Are you so foolish? Having *begun by the Spirit, are you now being perfected by the flesh?*" (3:3, emphasis added). If the Spirit's work of salvation is by grace alone, then our growth must be by grace alone as well. Spiritual disciplines put us in a better place to receive grace but make no mistake; they do not change a person. Only God's grace through the Holy Spirit can do that (cf., 1 Cor. 3:7). John Owen remarks:

> The Spirit alone reveals unto us the fullness of
> Christ for our relief...the Spirit alone establishes the

*heart in expectation of relief from Christ; which is
the great sovereign means of mortification...the
Spirit alone brings the cross of Christ into our
hearts with its sin-killing power; for by the Spirit
are we baptized into the death of Christ.[30]*

Spiritual change is accomplished with spiritual
measures. That is why grace must change us. Spiritual
measures mean depending upon God's gracious work of
the Holy Spirit to grow our faith and love in the crucified
One. This understanding is essential to tapping out sin.
Galatians 2:20 says:

*I have been crucified with Christ. It is no longer I who
live, but Christ who lives in me. And the life I now
live in the flesh I live <u>by faith in the Son of God, who
loved me and gave himself for me</u>.* (emphasis added)

How are you employing the spiritual disciplines in your
life? Are you letting them guide you back to Calvary so
that you might, once again, let the gospel grow your love
for Christ? Do you find your satisfaction with Christ on
the increase or decrease? Can you say you are using
spiritual disciplines to help you "live by faith in the Son of
God" or have they become formulaic ways to earn God's
favor? Are activities like Scripture, community, prayer and
fasting viewed as bread or barter? Make sure you are
pursing God's grace to fight sin in a grace-filled manner.

THE GOSPEL IS OUR GREAT HELP

Once we appropriate the glory of the gospel, we are then ready to do battle and truly tap sin out. Refreshingly, the Cross helps us to see that Christianity is not primarily about what I do for Jesus but what Jesus has done for me. One could even say it is about performance – God's performance in Christ on our behalf. And that good news is freeing: it frees us to fight sin knowing that we are forgiven and accepted no matter what happens!

Once you understand that belief, you can apply it to your behavior. Notice how Paul continues Romans 6. He began the chapter discussing our belief in the gospel, but now the apostle turns to the behavior that gospel-knowledge should produce:

> Let not sin therefore reign in your mortal body, to make you obey its passions. Do not present your members to sin as instruments for unrighteousness, but present yourselves to God as those who have been brought from death to life, and your members to God as instruments for righteousness. For sin will have no dominion over you, since you are not under law but under grace. (12-14)

To tap out sin, go to the gospel first with your sin. Fly to the Cross! Trust deeply that God in Christ has taken care of your sin, let that gospel truth empower you by the Holy Spirit and use the spiritual disciplines to feast upon the goodness of grace. To do so is to find help in the battle with sin like never before. If you would fight this

toughest of opponents and win, it seems only fitting to
pray a prayer of the Puritans:

O LORD GOD,
Thou hast commanded me to believe in Jesus;
and I would flee to no other refuge,
wash in no other fountain,
build on no other foundation,
receive from no other fullness,
rest in no other relief.
His water and blood were not severed
in their flow at the cross,
may they never be separated in my creed and experiences;
May I be equally convinced of the guilt
and pollution of sin,
feel my need of a prince and Saviour,
implore of him repentance as well as forgiveness,
love holiness, and be pure in heart,
have the mind of Jesus, and tread in his steps.
Let me not be at my own disposal,
but rejoice that I am under the care of one
who is too wise to err,
too kind to injure,
too tender to crush.
May I scandalize none by my temper and conduct, but
recommend and endear Christ to all around,
bestow good on every one as circumstances permit,
and decline no opportunity of usefulness.
Grant that I may value my substance,
not as the medium of pride and luxury,

but as the means of my support and stewardship.
Help me to guide my affections with discretion,
to owe no man anything,
to be able to give to him that needeth,
to feel it my duty and pleasure
to be merciful and forgiving,
to show to the world the likeness of Jesus.[31]

DISCUSSION QUESTIONS

1. What does *belief before behavior* mean and how does it apply to fighting sin? Why is it a critical strategy?
2. What does this statement mean? *The gospel isn't only for the unbeliever but also the believer.*
3. Based on Romans 6:6-11, how has the Christian been set free from sin?
4. Have you ever been told to simply *"do the disciplines"* in response to a struggle with a particular sin? How can this potentially be ineffective counsel?
5. How can spiritual disciplines become a trap of performance for the Christian? How do we keep from falling into that trap?
6. Why is the gospel central in fighting sin? How does it deal with the guilt of our sin?
7. What role does love play into defeating any particular sin? How does the gospel create grateful love in our heart and why is it is such an essential motivation of the spiritual disciplines?
8. What does it mean to "set your faith at work on Christ" when struggling in the cage with sin?
9. How does the truth of "no condemnation" (cf., Romans 8:1) for those in Christ make you feel? How should the goodness of grace impact our heart amidst the wins and losses in fighting temptation?
10. Why is it important to see our sanctification (our growth) rooted in our justification (being made right with God through Christ's redemptive work)?

CONCLUSION

Labor, therefore, to fill your hearts with the cross of Christ
...that there may be no room for sin.

– JOHN OWEN

L et me ask a question posed at the very beginning of this book: *Are you fighting sin hard, or are you fighting sin well?* You can do the former without the latter. Fighting sin well means taking your sin to the gospel first. It means revisiting the place where the battle over sin has been decided forever – the Cross. While Scripture memory, accountability and other spiritual disciplines are necessary for this fight, the gospel must precede and permeate those disciplines. There is no other path to real, lasting victory outside this gospel-centered approach. The Puritans knew this. John Owen knew this. We must know this. It is how we fight sin well.

I did not write this book because I knew how to easily beat sin. I wrote this book because I know where sin has been beaten! If anything, I have not learned how good I am at defeating sin (sometimes I am downright awful), but how soundly sin has been defeated on my behalf. Whether in victory or defeat, I am continually reminded of the supremacy of the Cross and how deeply I need to grow in my understanding of that gospel power.

I wrote this book because I frequently see well-meaning believers approach their sin with the same ineffective strategy I used for years, leaving them frustrated and fruitless for the cause of Christ. This does not mean a person who employs a gospel-centered approach will never lose to sin. He will, however, find more strength for the fight – a strength that may lead him to more victories than ever before. When he does succumb to sin, he will be more apt to find an enduring hope in a Savior who has succeeded for him where he has failed. He will be reminded that God has done for us in Christ what we could not do for ourselves. He will better understand the sweet truth that the gospel is our life. As Jonathan Edwards wrote, the gospel is "the true saint's superstructure."[32] That, my friend, is the mindset of every successful sin-fighter.

I must also add that I wrote this book because John Owen is worth reading. I think of this book as "Owen for those who won't read Owen." Indeed, I would plead with those who have remotely benefitted from *Tap* to consider reading Owen's "*Of the Mortification of Sin in Believers*". A wonderful edition by Kelly M. Kapic and Justin Taylor entitled *Overcoming Sin and Temptation* (Crossway, 2006) is available at the writing of this book. Finally, I would humbly suggest Owen's work would easily qualify as one of the profitable "old books" C.S. Lewis encourages

Christians to read, correcting the mistakes of our generation while delivering older truths that God in Christ desires that we not only live out, but fight from!

Fight well.

> *My sin, oh, the bliss of this glorious thought!*
> *My sin, not in part but the whole,*
> *is nailed to the cross, and I bear it no more,*
> praise *the Lord, praise the Lord, O my soul!*[33]

NOTES

Introduction

1. C.S. Lewis, *Introduction to Athanasius' On The Incarnation*, trans. By Sister Penelope Lawson, Anglican Community of St. Mary the Virgin in Wantage, England.

Chapter One: Life in the Cage

2. http://www.thefutoncritic.com/news.aspx?id=200610 11spiketv01, (accessed April 10, 2009).
3. http://the.honoluluadvertiser.com/article/2007/Mar/23/br/br7138 906254.html, (accessed April 10, 2009).
4. As cited in Jonathan Edwards, *The Religious Affections*, 321, fn.
5. John Owen, *Of The Mortification of Sin*, 10.

Chapter Two: Before You Enter the Cage

6. http://www.sportsnet.ca/mma/2009/06/30/showdown_mma_refs/, (accessed July 2009)
7. Owen, 34.
8. William Willimon, "Powerpoint Preaching", *Leadership Magazine*, Summer 2007, 34.

NOTES

Chapter Three: Holds That Don't Work

9. Richard Sibbes, *Bruised Reed*, VI.
10. Owen, 26.
11. Tim Keller, *The Luther Project*, www.redeemer.com

Chapter Four: Having a Good Hold

12. Owen, *Of the Mortification of Sin in Believers*, 32.
13. Ibid.

Chapter Five: Repenting of Repenting

14. http://www.palmbeachpost.com/sports/content/sports/ep
    aper/2008/10/05/1005mma.html, (accessed July 2009).
15. Tim Keller, *All of Life is Repentance*,
    www.redeemer.com
16. Owen, 72.
17. Jonathan Edwards, *The Religious Affections*, 278.

Chapter Six: Contender Repentance

18. Wayne Grudem, *Systematic Theology*, 490.
19. Timothy Keller, *Gospel Christianity I*, 37.
20. Thomas Watson, *The Doctrine of Repentance*, 40.
21. Matthew Mead, *The Almost Christian Discovered*, SDG, 32
22. Owen, 77.
23. Watson, 49.
24. Thomas Watson, *The Doctrine of Repentance*, np.

Chapter Seven: Tapping Out Sin

25. Augustus Toplady, *Rock of Ages*.

26. Illustrations are adapted from Jerry Bridges, *The Discipline of Grace*, 20-21.
27. Thomas Chalmers, sermon, *The Expulsive Power of a New Affection*.
28. John Owen, *Of the Mortification of Sin in Believers*, 85.
29. As heard quoted by Dr. Bryan Chapell at Covenant Seminary on May 25, 2010.
30. Owen, 86.
31. *Jesus My Glory, The Valley of Vision: A Collection of Puritan Prayers and Devotions*, 42-43.

Conclusion

32. Jonathan Edwards, <u>Religious Affections</u>, 176.
33. Horatio Spafford, *It is Well with My Soul*.

* Quote attributed to Hoyce Gracie in chapter 1 taken from http://www.reference.com/browse/Royce_Gracie, UFC 2 event, (accessed July 2010).

Quote attributed to Mark Coleman in chapter 2 taken from http://www.mmawild.com/ufc/quotes/, (accessed July 2009).

Quote by Georges St. Pierre in chapter 4 was transcribed from http://www.youtube.com/watch?v=Xx4r8oa7Z0U&eurl=http%3A%2F%2F, UFC 100 Pre-fight interview, (accessed July 2009).

AUTHOR

Yancey Arrington is the Teaching Pastor at Clear Creek Community Church in League City, Texas, a suburb of Houston, where he has served since 1998. He is husband to Jennefer and father to three sons; Thatcher, Haddon and Beckett. A native Texan, Yancey loves to spend time with family and friends at his ranch house in the Texas Hill Country. He is also an avid sports fan with a soft spot in his heart for the Houston Astros. Obviously, Yancey is learning much about patience and longsuffering.

He is a graduate of Baylor University (Religion, 1993), Southwestern Baptist Theological Seminary (Master of Divinity with Biblical Languages, 1996) and currently pursuing a Doctor of Ministry at Covenant Theological Seminary in St. Louis. You can find more of Yancey's thoughts and work at his blog, www.YanceyArrington.com, or follow him on Twitter at @yanceyarrington.

**BE KILLING SIN OR
IT WILL BE KILLING YOU.**

– JOHN OWEN

241.3 ARR

Arrington, Yancey.

Tap

OCT 2 0 2014